# Reform Capacity

**Johannes Lindvall** is a Professor of Political Science at Lund University, Sweden. He is the author of *Mass Unemployment and the State* (Oxford University Press 2010) as well as articles in journals such as the *American Political Science Review*, the *British Journal of Political Science*, *Comparative Political Studies*, the *European Journal of Political Research*, the *Journal of Politics*, and *World Politics*.

# Reform Capacity

Johannes Lindvall

OXFORD
UNIVERSITY PRESS

# OXFORD
UNIVERSITY PRESS

Great Clarendon Street, Oxford, OX2 6DP,
United Kingdom

Oxford University Press is a department of the University of Oxford.
It furthers the University's objective of excellence in research, scholarship,
and education by publishing worldwide. Oxford is a registered trade mark of
Oxford University Press in the UK and in certain other countries

© Johannes Lindvall 2017

The moral rights of the author have been asserted

First published 2017
First published in paperback 2019

Published in the United States of America by Oxford University Press
198 Madison Avenue, New York, NY 10016, United States of America

British Library Cataloguing in Publication Data
Data available

Library of Congress Cataloging in Publication Data
Data available

ISBN 978-0-19-876686-5 (Hbk.)
ISBN 978-0-19-884681-9 (Pbk.)

# Acknowledgments

This book is based on research that I have carried out over many years, alone and in collaboration with others. It was made possible by a grant from the European Research Council, which funded the project The Reform Capacity of Governments (Starting Grant 284313). I am deeply grateful to the three other members of the Reform Capacity team—Per Andersson, Thomas Brambor, and Carlo Knotz—for their contributions to the project. I am also grateful to the research assistants that worked with us over the years: Malin Bredenberg, Alvina Erman, Simon Kus, Moa Olin, Annika Stjernquist, and Anna Wilson.

Many colleagues and friends have offered help and advice along the way. I would especially like to mention Hans Agné, Karen Anderson, Ben Ansell, Michael Becher, Pablo Beramendi, Nancy Bermeo, Hanna Bäck, David Doyle, Ole Elgström, Vincenzo Galasso, John Gerring, Jane Gingrich, the late David Goldey, Peter Hall, Swen Hutter, Silja Häusermann, Torben Iversen, Desmond King, Victor Lapuente, Cathie Jo Martin, Iain McLean, Daniel Naurin, Bryn Rosenfeld, Bo Rothstein, David Rueda, Luis Schiumerini, Petra Schleiter, David Soskice, Carlos Scartascini, Jonas Tallberg, Jan Teorell, Mariano Tommasi, George Tsebelis, Maya Tudor, and Ann Towns. I am very grateful, as ever, to Carl Dahlström. I would also like to thank Dominic Byatt and three anonymous reviewers for Oxford University Press.

This book puts claims that I have made in previous work in context, developing a wide-ranging argument about the relationship between political institutions and the ability of governments to adopt and implement reforms. None of my published articles are incorporated *in extenso* in the book, but the book draws in part on earlier papers: "The Reform Capacity of Coalition Governments" (unpublished, 2009), "Power Sharing and Reform Capacity" (*Journal of Theoretical Politics* 22:3, 2010), "The Political Foundations of Trust and Distrust: Reforms and Protests in France" (*West European Politics* 34:2, 2011), "Union Density and Political Strikes" (*World Politics* 65:3, 2013), "Coalitions and Compensation: The Case of Unemployment Benefit Duration" (*Comparative Political Studies* 48:5, 2015, with Carlo Knotz), "Commitment Problems in Coalitions: A New Look at the Fiscal Policies of Multiparty Governments" (*Political Science Research and Methods* 3:1, 2015, with Hanna Bäck), "Fiscal Capacity, Domestic Compensation, and Trade Policy" (unpublished, 2015, with Thomas Brambor), and "Crises, Investments, and Institutions" (unpublished, 2016, with Per Andersson).

When this project began, I was a post-doctoral fellow at the University of Oxford. When it ended, I was teaching at Lund University. I am grateful to both institutions for their support.

My special thanks go to my family, especially to my wife, Johanna, and our two young sons, Otto and Ingemar. The boys are wild about Lin-Manuel Miranda's musical *Hamilton*, so I know that they will approve of the Alexander Hamilton quote on page 3.

# Contents

# Contents

# List of Figures

# List of Tables

# 1

# Two Theories of Effective Government

It is often said that effective government requires a concentration of power. If we want our political leaders to adjust public policies to changing economic, social, and political circumstances, adopting reforms that benefit society as a whole, we should, in this view, leave our leaders *alone*: we should put in place electoral procedures that identify a clear winner in each election, and then we should let the winning political party govern, until the next election, without having to cooperate with others. This idea, which I call the concentration-of-power hypothesis, has a long history in political thought. It is also implicit in day-to-day political commentary: multiparty governments, divided governments, and minority governments are frequently described as fragmented, or weak, or unable to get things done.

The concentration-of-power hypothesis is based on a simple and straightforward argument. Political parties that share power—within the executive, within the legislature, or across levels of government—often disagree with each other, and these disagreements sometimes keep governments from responding to important economic, social, and political problems. If reforms that benefit society as a whole can be blocked by a single party, because of that party's particular interests, the government as a whole may become ineffective or even paralyzed.

Notwithstanding the common-sense quality of this idea, I argue in this book that the concentration-of-power hypothesis is mistaken, since it seriously underestimates the ability of political decision-makers to overcome democratic paralysis by compensating losers (groups that stand to lose if a reform is implemented). If reforms benefit society as a whole, it must at least in principle be possible for the winners (those who benefit from a reform) to share some of their gains with the losers. This book shows that reform capacity—the ability of political decision-makers to adopt and implement policy changes that benefit society as a whole—can be achieved in two different ways. One method, which is consistent with the concentration-of-power hypothesis, is to build institutions that enable governments to *ignore* losers from reform. The other method, which governments rely more on in power-sharing systems, is to build institutions that enable governments to *compensate* losers from reform.

The book discusses numerous empirical examples of how governments have built support for reforms by compensating losers. These examples are drawn from several different policy areas, including trade policy and labor market policy (Chapter 2 onward), fiscal policy (Chapter 3), social policy (Chapter 4 and Chapter 5), and tax policy and economic policy (Chapter 5).

If political decision-makers are able to solve the bargaining problems that can sometimes complicate negotiations between winners and losers (I discuss those problems Chapter 3), power-sharing systems have certain *advantages* over power-concentration systems, since the inclusive reform strategies that governments rely on in power-sharing systems may enable governments to accomplish things they could not otherwise accomplish. Chapter 4 shows that power sharing can lead to high reform capacity in societies where interest groups operating outside the bounds of formal institutions are powerful enough to block reforms. Chapter 5 argues that power sharing can lead to high reform capacity when reforms have investment-like properties—short-term costs and long-term benefits—since it helps to correct some of the short-sightedness that is inherent in democratic policymaking.

These are radical arguments, since they cast doubt on the common view that reform capacity is always higher in power-concentration systems than in power-sharing systems. The question whether political power should be concentrated or shared is one of the oldest questions in comparative politics, and the choice between these two types of institutions is typically described as a trade-off. Power-concentration institutions are associated with decisiveness and accountability. Power-sharing institutions are associated with the political virtues of representativeness and democratic deliberation. Arend Lijphart has long argued, for instance, that "consensual" democracies are superior to "majoritarian" democracies since they are "kinder" and "gentler," protecting minorities and forcing policymakers to take many different views into account before they adopt new policies (Lijphart 2012, Chapter 16). Bingham Powell argues, similarly, that the proportional "vision" of democracy is associated with more representative government than the majoritarian "vision," since the policies that political decision-makers adopt in proportional systems bear a closer resemblance to the policies that the median voter desires (Powell 2000, Chapters 8 and 9). Political economists such as Witold Henisz (2000, 2004) and Irfan Nooruddin (2011) argue, meanwhile, that although decision-making may be slower in power-sharing systems, this slowness is actually advantageous since it leads to a more secure business environment, encouraging investments and growth.

My objection to the concentration-of-power hypothesis is different. Like a few other recent studies (notably Tommasi et al. 2014), this book is a direct attack on the idea that power sharing slows down reform in the first place.[1]

Reform capacity is an important element of good government. Alexander Hamilton was right to argue, long ago, that we should be motivated by a "zeal for the firmness and efficiency of government" (Hamilton 2003 [1787], 3). But in modern states, concentrating power in the hands of the executive is not the only way to achieve this goal.

## The Problem of Reform Capacity

The problems that governments confront today are rarely the same problems that governments confronted one, two, or three decades ago. Economic conditions change rapidly, due to technological innovations and shifting patterns of production, consumption, and trade. Social norms and practices evolve. Political conditions also change, as a result of shifting geopolitical threats and the unforeseen effects of past political decisions.

Since society is in constant flux, the policies that governments adopted ten, twenty, or thirty years ago are not necessarily equipped to solve today's problems. If political decision-makers fail to reform public policies by adapting them to new economic, social, and political circumstances, the policies that we have inherited from past governments therefore tend to become less effective over time—inaction leads to "drift," a "politically driven failure of public policies to adapt to the shifting realities of a dynamic economy and society" (Hacker and Pierson 2010, 170; Callander and Krehbiel 2014, 821).

I use the term "reform capacity" to describe the relationship between political institutions and the ability of political decision-makers to adjust public policies to changing economic, social, and political circumstances by adopting and implementing policy changes that benefit society as a whole. In political science, the word "reform" is often used as shorthand for a big change in public policy. My own definition comes closer to the word's everyday meaning, which is the "action or process of making changes in an institution, organization, or aspect of social or political life, so as to remove errors, abuses, or other hindrances to proper performance" (*Oxford English Dictionary*). It also comes close to the standard usage in economics, where

---

[1] See also Gehlbach and Malesky (2010) and McGann and Latner (2013). Lijphart questions the idea of a trade-off between reform capacity and other goals on empirical grounds (Lijphart 2012, Chapter 15).

reform is typically taken to mean "the adoption of a superior policy" (Drazen 2000, 405).[2]

The question of what makes certain policies "superior" (and, conversely, when policies become "hindrances to proper performance") is difficult to answer, and it cannot be answered fully without considering problems of political philosophy that fall outside the scope of this book.

But I proceed on the assumption that there are some goals, such as economic prosperity and national security, that most people would agree are desirable. I also take for granted—and this is perhaps a less controversial claim—that there are some harms, such as deep economic crises and environmental degradation, that most people believe should be avoided. In other words, I will simply assume, for now, that it is in principle possible to distinguish between policy choices that are "zero-sum" (what one group wins, another must lose) and policy choices that are "positive-sum" (on balance, the positive effects outweigh the negative effects). If the government's choice is zero-sum and the government adopts a new policy, some people will be better off, and others will be worse off, but society as a whole will be neither worse off nor better off. If the government's choice is positive-sum and the government adopts a new policy, many people will be better off and only a few people will be worse off, or some people will be much better off and others will be only slightly worse off (only rarely will a policy change make *everyone* better off).

By "better off," I do not necessarily mean *financially* better off. Most of the reforms that I discuss in the book are economic reforms, such as trade reforms (which are meant to increase national income), labor market reforms (which are meant to reduce unemployment and increase employment), debt-reduction programs (which are meant to bring down government debt), and economic stabilization plans (which are meant to avert a collapse in economic activity). But that is only because economic reforms provide interesting examples of the sorts of political conflicts that I wish to examine. There are other ways to make people better off (by introducing environmental regulations that reduce pollution, for instance). Generally, a policy change qualifies as a "reform" if it is intended to achieve some economic, social, or political improvement that most people would welcome (economic prosperity, a clean environment), or, alternatively, if it is intended to mitigate some harm that most people believe should be avoided (mounting government debt, a sharp economic downturn).

In a political system with a high level of reform capacity, political conflicts among parties, factions, or interest groups do not keep governments

---

[2] I should note that I have used the term "reform" in the less precise sense of "big change in policy" in my own work (see, for example, Lindvall and Sebring 2005).

from adopting and implementing policy changes that are widely seen as desirable, or even necessary. Many metaphors have been used to describe the *opposite* of reform capacity: "gridlock" (a traffic metaphor), "logjam" (a lumber metaphor), "stalemate" (a chess metaphor). Following Kenneth Arrow (1963, 120), and following contemporary commentary on the collapse of the Fourth Republic in France (Domenach 1958), I prefer the medical metaphor "democratic paralysis" (which Arrow defined as "a failure to act due not to a desire for inaction but an inability to agree on the proper action").[3]

The reason that reforms are not always adopted, even if they benefit society as whole, is that some people almost always lose, and if the losers are powerful enough, they have strong incentives to block reforms. Trade reforms typically increase national income, but they nevertheless harm some sectors of the economy (and, in the long run, if Stolper and Samuelson are to be believed, some factors of production). Some labor market reforms do reduce structural employment, as the labor economics literature suggests they should, but they do so by making life harder for the unemployed. And although fiscal consolidation programs often reduce government debt, they always involve tax increases and expenditure cuts that harm some groups more than others. The "losers" may well gain something from a reform—no one benefits from having an unsustainable level of government debt, for instance—but their losses are greater, sometimes far greater, than their gains. That is what it means to be a loser.

Since the problem of reform is closely related with the problem of political conflict, we can define reform capacity more precisely as the highest level of conflict that a political system can tolerate before political decision-makers cease to adopt policy changes that benefit society as a whole. When reform capacity is low, democratic paralysis is endemic: all sorts of minor political disagreements result in inaction. When reform capacity is high, governments are able to adopt and implement significant reforms even if political conflicts are deep-seated and divisive.[4]

## Concentrating or Sharing Power

The idea that effective government requires a concentration of power goes back to predemocratic times. Poland's geopolitical decline in the

---

[3] I avoid the term "ungovernability," which was central to many analyses of political malaise in the 1970s and 1980s (see especially Crozier et al. 1975), since the meaning of that term is often vague, ambiguous, or both (Rose 1979).

[4] Häusermann (2010) uses the term "reform capacity" in a related but not identical sense: for Häusermann, reform capacity is the ability to adopt "modernizing" reforms. Two other books that I am aware of, Featherstone and Papadimitriou (2008) and Andersen, Bergman, and Jensen (2015), also use the term.

early-modern period, for example, is often attributed to the fragmentation of political power in the Polish polity (Finer 1997, Volume III, Section 8.5.3).

The version of the concentration-of-power hypothesis that concerns us here, however, is the claim that certain forms of representative *democracy* increase the risk of political paralysis. This idea can be found already in nineteenth-century critiques of continental Europe's emerging representative systems, such as Henry Sumner Maine's *Popular Government* (1885) and Lawrence Lowell's *Governments and Parties in Continental Europe* (1896). But the notion that power sharing in general and proportional representation in particular are associated with ineffective government became especially prominent in the interwar years. As William Riker (1984, 25) has noted, the disaffection with proportional representation and multiparty government in that period was a direct result of political developments in Italy's constitutional monarchy in the early 1920s and in the Weimar Republic in Germany in the 1920s and early 1930s. Many scholars and political commentators—notably Herman Finer (*The Case Against Proportional Representation*, 1924, 1935) and Ferdinand Hermens (*Democracy or Anarchy?*, 1941)—concluded that the breakdown of democracy in Italy and Germany resulted from the weakness of Italian and German coalition governments.[5] Joseph Schumpeter was opposed to proportional representation for similar reasons, arguing that "it may prevent democracy from producing efficient governments and thus prove a danger in times of stress" (1942, 272).[6]

Multiparty government is one important form of power sharing, but it is not the only one. I use the term broadly, referring to all democratic systems in which executive power, legislative power, or both are divided among several political parties. Like Moe and Caldwell (1994, 182), who emphasize the similarities between multiparty parliamentary systems and presidential separation-of-powers systems, such as the United States; like Tsebelis (2002), who analyzes all different forms of power sharing using the concept of "veto players"; and like Lijphart (1984, 1999, 2012), who distinguishes between "consensual" and "majoritarian" democracies, I start by treating all forms of power sharing as essentially similar.

Later on, I will show that there are important differences between different forms of power sharing, since political decision-makers need to solve

---

[5] When a new edition of his anti-proportional-representation treatise *Democracy or Anarchy?* was released in the 1970s, Ferdinand Hermens maintained that proportional representation undermined democracy and suggested that the apparent success of proportional representation in Western Europe in the post-war period was a "fair weather" phenomenon (Hermens 1972, 445).

[6] Note that according to Schumpeter, all the positive arguments for proportional representation are themselves flawed (the purpose of democratic elections, in Schumpeter's view, is to identify a leader that the electorate can accept, not to aggregate preferences). He therefore did not think that it was necessary to conduct a careful examination of the risks associated with proportional representation.

different problems in different systems. This is why most of the empirical examples that I discuss in the book are concerned with specific forms of power sharing, especially coalition government, and not with power sharing in general. For now, however, we can treat the distinction between power-concentration systems and power-sharing systems as equivalent to the distinction between what Bingham Powell (2000) calls the "majoritarian" and the "proportional" visions of democracy. As Powell has demonstrated, rules about elections and rules about political decision-making are highly correlated in democracies: where power is more dispersed in the early stages of the political process (the appointment of political office-holders), it is typically also dispersed in later stages (decision-making). In ideal-typical "majoritarian" systems, Powell shows, the electoral procedures make it more likely that a single party will be able to control the executive, and the legislative procedures concentrate power in the executive, relieving the government of the burden of having to negotiate with other parties (Powell 2000, Chapter 2). In ideal-typical "proportional" systems, by contrast, the electoral procedures make it more likely that government formation will involve negotiations among several parties, and the legislative procedures disperse power, making it necessary for governments to consult with opposition parties before getting legislation adopted.

The British constitution provides an extreme example of power concentration (Lijphart 2012, Chapter 2). In the democratic era, the United Kingdom has only had coalition governments during brief periods (most recently in 2010–15): in almost every election, one party has won a clear majority of the seats in the House of Commons, enabling that party to form a single-party government. Meanwhile, the ruling party's power is less constrained by other institutions than in other democracies.

Switzerland provides an extreme example of power sharing (Lijphart 2012, Chapter 3). Switzerland's government, the Federal Council, is a semipermanent coalition of the four major parties: the liberal FDP (*Die Liberalen* in German), the Christian democratic CVP (*Christlichdemokratische Volkspartei*), the agrarian-turned-far-right SVP (*Schweizerische Volkspartei*), and the center-left SPS (*Sozialdemokratische Partei der Schweiz*). These four parties have divided the seven cabinet seats among themselves since the late 1950s (and by that time, Switzerland had *already* been governed by a semi-permanent coalition of parties since the late nineteenth century) (Ladner 2004).

I only use the term power sharing to refer to the division of executive or legislative power among political parties and politicians. I do not treat constitutional courts (or appellate courts with the power of judicial review, such as the United States Supreme Court) as instances of power sharing, since judges have narrow, well-defined tasks and do not bargain over public policy. For the same reasons, I do not treat the delegation of policymaking competencies to central banks (Cukierman 1992) or to autonomous government agencies (Jordana et al. 2011) as instances of power sharing. Finally, I do not treat corporatism—the delegation of political power to interest organizations—as a form of power sharing. There is a strong correlation between corporatism and the structure of party competition (Lijphart and Crepaz 1991; Hamann and Kelly 2007; Baccaro and Simoni 2008; Martin and Swank 2008, 2011; Anthonsen and Lindvall 2009), so we can think of corporatism as an extension of power sharing among political parties, not as a form of power sharing in its own right.

Judicial review, bureaucratic delegation, and corporatism feature prominently in this book—especially in Chapter 3—but they feature as explanatory factors, not as instances of power sharing.

Judging from contemporary academic and political discourse, the concentration-of-power hypothesis continues to enjoy broad support among scholars, intellectuals, and politicians. For instance, Torsten Persson and Guido Tabellini (2006, 734) claim in one survey article that a "large number of veto players tends to 'lock in' economic policy and reduce its ability to respond to shocks" (see also Persson and Tabellini 2003). In another survey article, dealing with the effects of political institutions on political "performance," Manfred G. Schmidt (2002, 150) makes a similar claim: "Challenges requiring . . . rapid decision making tend to overburden the non-majoritarian democracies." He concludes that in such systems, the capacity to "design and implement significant policy changes" is often lacking. "Due to the large number of participants in policy deliberation and decision making, non-majoritarian democracies usually need longer periods of time to reach a consensus or initiatives may even get stuck in a blocked decision-making process."[7]

The most influential book on the relationship between institutions and political decision-making in recent decades is George Tsebelis's *Veto Players* (2002). Tsebelis's book, which has had a powerful impact in political science and related disciplines, builds on a series of earlier papers (1995; 1999; 2000) and has been extended in subsequent studies (notably the contributions to the book edited by König et al. in 2010).

Tsebelis argues that "policy stability," which is defined as the impossibility of significant policy changes, "will be the result of large coalition governments, particularly if the coalition partners have significant ideological differences among them" (Tsebelis 1999, 591). More generally, Tsebelis argues that governments have more room for maneuver in systems with few "partisan"

[7] In his book *Constitutional Engineering*, Giovanni Sartori argues, similarly, that coalition governments are only able to govern well if the number of parties in government is small and coalitions are "coalescent" rather than "conflictual" (1997, 58); if these conditions are not met, Sartori suggests, coalition governments are unable to handle their internal divisions.

and "institutional" veto players than in systems with many veto players. Tsebelis's book, which contributes to a larger literature on the role of "veto points" and "veto power" in political decision-making (see, for instance, Immergut 1992, Huber et al. 1993, and Cox and McCubbins 2001), thus provides a theoretical justification for the concentration-of-power hypothesis.

Tsebelis's book does not say whether it is a good thing or a bad thing to have many veto players. In fact, Tsebelis writes explicitly that it is not his goal "to make a statement about which institutions are better" (Tsebelis 2002, 1). The reason, as Tsebelis explains elsewhere, is that "sometimes policy stability is desirable; at other times policy change is necessary" (Tsebelis 2000, 443). But Tsebelis's argument about the relationship between political institutions and political decision-making does imply that reform capacity, as I define it here, should be lower in political systems where power is shared among several veto players than in political systems where power is concentrated. Indeed, in one of his papers Tsebelis states clearly that high policy stability will "make the change of even an undesirable status quo difficult" (Tsebelis 2000, 443).

My view is that it is a mistake to apply the veto-player model to the problem of reform capacity.

The main difference between Tsebelis's theory of veto players and the argument of this book is that my argument allows for compensatory side payments to losers from reform. Tsebelis's theory, by contrast, is based on the assumption that political agents cannot make side payments. He writes that although he does not want to argue that side payments are always impossible, they should not be introduced "as a constant feature of the analysis" since that would make all outcomes possible and theories of political decision would become impossible to test (Tsebelis 2002, 285). In a more recent paper, Tsebelis notes again that "[t]he reason that such explanations are not discussed very much in the literature (including the veto players book) is because such explanations (if accepted) would explain everything: for every instance of deviant behaviour there is a price (either in money or in policy) that can explain the deviation, and consequently, any behaviour can be explained" (Tsebelis 2010).

This is a serious challenge (my answer can be found in Chapter 3 of this book). But if bargaining over compensation and side payments is a crucial part of what politicians *do* in power-sharing systems, as I think it is, then a theory of political decision-making that excludes the possibility of compensatory side payments is severely limited.

The most outspoken *critic* of the concentration-of-power hypothesis in contemporary political science, Arend Lijphart, has argued since the 1960s that the "consensual" model of democracy has many virtues that the "majoritarian" model lacks, and that the virtues of the majoritarian model are often exaggerated (Lijphart 1968, 1984, 1999, 2012). There are two principal differences between my own approach and that of Lijphart (and his followers). The first difference, as I mentioned in the introduction to this chapter, is that my argument is a *direct* attack on the idea that power sharing leads to democratic paralysis. Lijphart has suggested that "the greater speed and decisiveness of majoritarian government are more apparent than real" (Lijphart 1977, 118; see also Lijphart 2012, Chapter 15), but his main argument in favor of power sharing is that consensus democracy has other virtues, such as a greater capacity for deliberation and a more "steady" policymaking style (see especially Lijphart 2012, Chapter 16). The second difference is that the outcome variables that interest me are policy *choices* (the decisions that politicians make); the outcome variables that interest Lijphart, by contrast, are policy *outcomes* (the economic, social, and political "performance" of democracies).

This brings me to a more general point. There is an important difference between this book—which studies how different types of democracies solve, or fail to solve, the specific problem of reform—and the more general literature on democratic "performance." In addition to Lijphart, several other authors, such as Bueno de Mesquita et al. (2003), Roller (2005), Hall and Lamont (2009), Gerring and Thacker (2010), Rothstein (2011), Besley and Persson (2011), and Acemoglu and Robinson (2012), have recently conducted wide-ranging theoretical and empirical analyses of the effects of political institutions on economic and social outcomes such as human development, economic growth, public health, and political violence. My book is both more ambitious and less ambitious than these books. It is *more* ambitious since it provides a theoretical and empirical account of how democracies deal with a particular problem, whereas most of the books cited above examine macro-level correlations between institutional configurations and economic and social outcomes. But my book is also *less* ambitious, for it does not seek to answer general questions about the overall quality of democratic institutions; it asks specific questions about how democratic institutions influence certain types of conflicts.[8]

The previous study that comes *closest* to what this book seeks to do is Pablo Spiller's and Mariano Tommasi's *The Institutional Foundations of Public Policy in Argentina* (2009). The "transactions approach" that Spiller and Tommasi propose is close in spirit to some of the arguments that I develop in this book. But the theoretical ideas that inform my argument are different, in many respects, from Spiller and Tommasi's approach (which is more firmly grounded in transaction-cost economics). In particular, my book, unlike Spiller and Tommasi's, provides a detailed analysis of the problem of

---

[8] I discuss how the ideas and evidence that I present in this book contribute to the broader discussion about democratic performance in Chapter 6.

compensation. Moreover, the empirical examples that Spiller and Tommasi draw on are Latin American (see also the case studies included in Stein and Tommasi 2008, which builds on a similar theoretical model of political exchange), whereas the main geographical focus of my study is Western Europe and English-speaking former settler colonies in North America and the Asia-Pacific region.[9]

## Institutions and Conflicts

*[handwritten margin note: Reform capacity as maximum polarable conflict]*

I have defined reform capacity as the highest level of conflict that a political system can tolerate before political decision-makers cease to adopt and implement policy changes that benefit society as a whole. I have also argued that if governments can build support for reforms by compensating "losers," reform capacity does not necessarily require a concentration of power. It is true that one of the methods that governments use when they wish to adopt controversial reforms—*ignoring* the losers—is more rarely available to political decision-makers in power-sharing systems, but there is an alternative method—*compensating* the losers—that is at least in principle available to all governments.

Before I develop these ideas further, I would like to say a little more about what this book does and does not do, taking the definition of reform capacity as a starting point.

First of all, I concentrate on the role of conflict since I am assuming that politics is not harmonious: political decision-makers do not care about general welfare *per se*. They adopt policies that benefit society as a whole

---

[9] My book is also related to other recent studies that have questioned the idea that having a large number of veto players leads to a lower likelihood of policy change. I am thinking in particular of Tommasi et al. (2014), which argues on the basis of a repeated-games analysis of political decision-making that there is no contradiction between "decisiveness" and "resoluteness" (see also Chapter 5); Gehlbach and Malesky (2010), which examines economic reforms in postcommunist states, finding that under certain conditions, special interests become less powerful when the number of veto players grows, increasing the likelihood of policy change; Szakonyi and Urpelainen (2014), which argues on the basis of an analysis of the regulation of utilities in different countries that the effect of the number of veto players on policy change varies depending on whether the government values political control; and McGann and Latner (2013), which argues on the basis of a social-choice model that far from being prone to paralysis, what they call "PR-majority rule" is in fact the most flexible form of democracy (they also test this argument empirically using cross-national data on government spending and welfare-state reform, finding that the veto-player model performs badly). There are also several examples of recent empirical studies that have produced findings that are clearly at odds with the concentration-of-power hypothesis; for example, Bernecker (2014), in a recent study of welfare reforms in the United States, finds that divided government (that is, power sharing between Democrats and Republicans within state governments) is associated with a higher, not lower, likelihood of welfare reform. Finally, my book is related to work on the nature and politics of "compensation" in other social science disciplines, notably Michael Trebilcock's recent book *Dealing With Losers* (2014).

because it is sometimes in their interest to do so (since they can distribute enough of the benefits of those reforms to their own supporters).

More generally, I assume throughout this book that political parties and interest groups act rationally and strategically to achieve their own political objectives (especially the welfare of the groups they represent). Consequently, my analysis pays almost no attention to *psychological* barriers to political compromises (Ross and Ward 1995), to political *learning* ("collectively wondering what to do"; Heclo 1974, 305), or to the formation of political preferences through democratic *deliberation* (see, for example, Elster 1998). The justification for these strong assumptions is that I wish to stack the deck in favor of the concentration-of-power hypothesis (and, therefore, against my own ideas). Many other scholars have sought to explain the performance of power-sharing systems with reference to other-regardingness, learning, and deliberation (Crepaz 1996; Birchfield and Crepaz 1998; Lijphart 2012, Chapter 16). I wish to show that it is possible to reach the conclusion that reform capacity can be high in power-sharing systems on the basis of a stylized rational-choice model of policymaking.

Another key element of my definition is that reform capacity is defined *ex ante*, not *ex post*. A theory of reform capacity that can only evaluate a political system's level of reform capacity *ex post*, once reforms have or have not happened, is analytically suspect and empirically useless. My definition of reform capacity avoids this problem. The term denotes the prerequisites of reform, not the adoption and implementation of actual reforms. Assuming that the magnitude of political conflicts can be observed, and assuming that the relationship between institutions and conflicts is well-understood, my definition makes it possible to define and describe a political system's level of reform capacity before the fact. The empirical analyses that I present in Chapters 2–5 rely, of course, on evidence about the actual adoption (or nonadoption) of particular policies, but the objective of these analyses is to make inferences about underlying levels of reform capacity in different systems.

Related to this, my definition treats reform capacity as a property of political *systems*. Consequently, my theory is mainly concerned with the underlying relationship between institutions, political conflicts, and reforms, and not with other parts of the policy process. One important literature in political science is concerned with the strategies that politicians use to make controversial and unpopular policy decisions more palatable to voters (see, for example, Pierson and Weaver 1993, Cox 2001, and Vis 2009). This book, by comparison, says little about the interaction between political parties and the electorate. Like Tsebelis's *Veto Players*, my book analyzes strategic interactions among a given set of political decision-makers. In Chapters 3 and 5, I consider the implications of upcoming elections for political decisions, but the elections are treated as stochastic events (I am not analyzing the preferences and behavior of individual voters or groups of voters).[10]

My definition of reform capacity is also based on the assumption that there are *levels* of political conflict, or, in other words, that political conflicts can be treated as matters of degree. This assumption is critical, for if political conflicts are absolute, there can be no compromise, and if there is no compromise, there can be no compensation. The theory only applies, therefore, to conflicts over "divisible" objects—a premise that my argument has in common with the rational theories of war that inspired it (Fearon 1995, 381–2).

Using the terminology that Avishai Margalit (2010) proposes in his book *On Compromise and Rotten Compromises*, this assumption makes my theory relevant for the *economic* view of politics, but not for the *religious* view. Margalit writes that "in the economic picture of politics everything is subject to compromise," but in the religious picture, "there are things over which we must never compromise" since "politics is a domain of human activity meant to protect a way of life and give meaning to human life" (Margalit 2010, 24). Margalit argues that most of us are motivated by both "economic" and "religious" considerations, which means that "[t]hose who lack stereoscopic vision—the perception of depth that comes from the use of both eyes—look at the political world with a single eye" (Margalit 2010, 148).[11]

How limited is the scope of my theory, given that it is mainly relevant for the economic view of politics? Many people clearly think about politics "religiously": they deal in absolutes, and do not live in the cost–benefit world of relative judgments. I would like to suggest as a plausible hypothesis, however, that religious views of politics tend to emerge as a reaction to unresponsive political systems. In European politics, for instance, one political division that separated "economic" from "religious" political dispositions is the historical split between reformist social democracy and revolutionary communism. Very crudely, social democrats have a pragmatic, "economic" view of politics, seeking stepwise political change through compromise, whereas communists have a radical, "religious" view of politics, seeking revolutionary change through uncompromising class struggle. As Stefano Bartolini shows in *The Political Mobilization of the European Left* (2000), the explanation for this split was at least in part institutional and political: a significant communist split only occurred where the socialist movement was characterized by "weak organization," "poor institutional integration," and

---

[10] My book is also only indirectly concerned with the role of reform-triggering events, such as economic crises (see Keeler 1993b and Drazen and Grilli 1993).

[11] As Ryan (2016, 409) shows, using individual-level data, "moralized" political attitudes "lead citizens to oppose compromises, punish compromising politicians, and forsake material gains" since such attitudes reorient behavior from "maximizing gains" to "adhering to rules." Note that Ryan observes that this tendency exists with respect to *both* economic and noneconomic issues, although he uses the term "economic" in a different way than Margalit.

13

"low political coalition potential" (Bartolini 2000, 542), especially in societies where the state's reaction to left-wing political mobilization was characterized by suppression and persecution. In such circumstances, Bartolini notes that "[t]he argument that no substantive political goals could be achieved without radical breakthroughs was convincing." The mix of "economic" and "religious" issues in a given political system is arguably not a natural fact, but a consequence of political structures and historical events (see also Fearon 1995, 382).

As I have already discussed, my definition of reform capacity also limits the scope of the theory to policy changes that *benefit society as a whole* (since compensatory side payments are only possible if a reform generates a "surplus"). My arguments assume, in other words, that it is at least in principle possible to distinguish between "zero-sum" and "positive-sum" conflicts, although it is often difficult to make this distinction in practice. I will say more about the normative considerations behind this assumption in the section "Expediency and Justice."

I end *this* section by noting that my definition anticipates a theoretical and empirical analysis of when, as a result of political conflicts, political decision-makers "cease" to adopt and implement desirable reforms. From the outset, therefore, I heed Tsebelis's warning that if we allow for the possibility of side payments without explaining when they are possible and when they are not, theoretical models of political decision-making become indeterminate, and therefore useless. We know that political decision-makers do not always overcome democratic paralysis by compensating the losers, so it is not enough to demonstrate that compensation is *possible*; it is necessary to also identify the *conditions* that make it so. The theoretical argument that I develop in this book pays a great deal of attention to this problem.

## Expediency and Justice

Reforms are policy changes that benefit society as a whole. But most reforms nevertheless harm some people. This raises a moral question: When is it justified to harm the few to help the many? It also raises a more practical, analytical question: What criterion should we use when distinguishing between positive-sum policy changes (reforms) and zero-sum policy changes (which merely make some people better off and other people worse off)?

I begin with the second question. The criterion that I rely on is the Kaldor–Hicks criterion of social welfare (Hicks 1939; Kaldor 1939), which is based on the idea that a policy change can (only) be said to have benefits for society if it is at least in principle possible to "compensate the losers at a cost to those favoured that falls short of their total gain" (Scitovszky 1941, 88).

In other words, if there is some policy that could at least potentially be used to redistribute some of the benefits of a reform to compensate the "losers," the reform satisfies the Kaldor–Hicks criterion (regardless of whether the losers are actually compensated). The idea behind this criterion is to separate the issue of efficiency (which can be estimated with empirical methods) from the issue of fairness (which cannot be estimated with empirical methods). If it is possible to compensate losers, the Kaldor–Hicks criterion treats a reform as efficient. Whether it is also morally justified is a different question, which needs to be analyzed separately.

As I explained in the section "Institutions and Conflicts," I have chosen to start from a stylized rational-choice model of policymaking since I wish to stack the deck against my own ideas about how political institutions work. I rely on the Kaldor–Hicks criterion for similar reasons. If I had chosen to rely on the so-called Pareto criterion, according to which a reform only improves social welfare if it benefits some people without harming *anyone*, I would have been much less likely to find that power-sharing institutions are associated with low levels of reform capacity.[12]

But we cannot treat the Kaldor–Hicks criterion as a general principle of political morality (nor, I think, did Hicks or Kaldor intend for it be used in this way). As Kenneth Arrow (1963, 34) notes, it is not debatable that a reform that meets the Kaldor–Hicks criterion should be seen as an unequivocal improvement over the status quo if the losers *are in fact compensated*, but it is not at all clear that such a policy should be preferred over the status quo if the compensation is *not actually paid* (Arrow 1963, 38). How we should think about the second case depends crucially on who the losers are, and on the manner in which they are harmed. Imagine, for instance, that the government would like to implement a reform that would make most people better off, but would harm some people who are already very poor; in these circumstances, forcing a reform on the losers without adequate compensation would bring to mind the prophet Nathan's parable of the rich man's slaughter of the poor man's lamb in Chapter 12 of the Second Book of Samuel.

Since the Kaldor–Hicks criterion cannot be treated as a general principle of political morality, we cannot treat reform capacity as the *first* virtue of

---

[12] It is true that I would have been even more likely to find in favor of the concentration-of-power hypothesis if I had used a purely utilitarian criterion. For the utilitarian reformers of the eighteenth and nineteenth centuries, a government policy should be adopted if the "tendency it has to augment the happiness of the community is greater than any which it has to diminish it" (Bentham 1823 [1780], iii). This criterion would be more favorable still to the concentration-of-power hypothesis since a policy change that makes many people better and a few people worse off would count as a reform even if it is not even in principle possible to compensate the losers. The Kaldor–Hicks criterion is a reasonable compromise, however—especially since it allows us to separate the question of the costs of compensation from the question of whether compensation is even possible, which will be helpful later on.

political institutions, and my arguments for the importance of reform capacity should not be interpreted thus. As John Rawls (1971, 1) observed, *justice* is the first virtue of social institutions. Living under a government that respects human and civil rights and liberties (as specified, for instance, by Rawls's first principle of justice) is certainly more important than reform capacity. So, I would argue, are the rule of law, political equality (and, consequently, democracy as such; see Beitz 1989), the impartiality of political institutions and integrity of public officials (Rothstein and Teorell 2008), and distributive fairness (which is the object of Rawls's second principle of justice).

But avoiding democratic paralysis is and remains an important goal of institution-building. Democratic paralysis is not only costly in terms of general welfare; it also has indirect, pernicious consequences for the legitimacy of democratic government. As Jane Mansbridge has recently argued (2012), "getting things done" is necessary for democratic legitimacy, since the phenomenon that Hacker and Pierson (2010) and Callander and Krehbiel (2014) call "drift" reduces the public's faith in political leaders and political institutions. Larry Diamond (1990, 49) has suggested, similarly, that "governability" is essential for democracy since all political systems "must always be able to act, and at times must do so quickly and decisively."

There is a flip side to the argument that most of us would think it unjust to adopt and implement a reform without compensating the losers if the losers are poor: if the losers are not at all poor, but belong to privileged social groups, we may not think that they *deserve* compensation.

When analyzing this problem, it is important to separate the question of whether compensation is politically expedient from the question of whether compensation is ethically desirable (Dixit and Londregan 1995, 856). These two problems are distinct. Compensation is often provided because it is politically expedient, not because it is desirable. Losers from reform, as I define them in this book, are only losers in the basic sense that they would be harmed relative to the status quo if a reform were adopted. Losers from reform are not necessarily harmed in a deeper, moral sense.

The difference between expediency and justice is brought home by the fact that compensation was used as a political strategy when the slave trade was abolished in Britain's dominions in the 1830s (for a longer discussion of the example of slavery, see Trebilcock 2014, Chapters 1 and 10). In 1833, the British government adopted a program of so-called "compensated emancipation," setting aside twenty million pounds to compensate slave owners in British possessions in the West Indies when slavery was banned there. The great American abolitionist William Lloyd Garrison, who was traveling in England at the time, wrote that this decision was "justly viewed as money bestowed where no loss can be proved" (quoted in Kellow 2007, 203). What Garrison meant by "loss," then, was to be robbed of something that one justly owns or deserves. Compensating slave owners can be perceived as an implicit acknowledgement that the slave owners were entitled to their slaves (for a discussion, see the contributions to Appiah and Bunzl 2007). Instead of compensating the slave owners, doing what is politically expedient in the short run, the right thing to do might have been to try to change the distribution of power in society, weakening the losers and making them powerless to resist reform in the long run. That is, in a sense, what happened in the United States, which did *not* opt for a strategy of compensated emancipation—although this solution to the conflict between northern and southern states was suggested by prominent politicians, such as the fourth President of the United States, James Madison (Fladeland 1976)—and where the conflict over slavery resulted in a civil war in the first half of the 1860s. But the benefits of the noncompensation strategy should be weighed against the great human costs of the Civil War (and against the cost of ending slavery as late as 1863).

The point that expediency and justice are different things is also brought home by the literature on corruption. It can be politically effective to use compensation to keep corrupt officials from obstructing public-sector reform (see Rose-Ackerman 1999, 198–9; for a more recent study, using historical data from Sweden, see Sundell 2014). Clearly, public-sector reform does not deprive corrupt officials of any legitimate income opportunities, so officials are not harmed in a meaningful, moral sense. Nevertheless, compensation is, in many circumstances, one of the most expedient methods of fighting corruption that are available to governments.

The observation that compensation does not always go to those we think deserve it is one of the main points of Sebastián Etchemendy's work on the politics of compensation in the Spanish-speaking democracies. Etchemendy notes that although the word "compensation" typically evokes support for the poor and the weak, this was not always what compensation meant in the Latin American context in the period that he studied. Etchemendy writes that the Argentine experience "reveals the significance of payoffs targeted to the powerful collective actors entrenched in the old state-centered system" (Etchemendy 2001, 3); compensation was not oriented to the economically weak, but to the politically strong.

## The Choices We Face

Each of the chapters that follow moves back and forth between theoretical ideas and empirical examples.

I state all theoretical arguments informally in the main text. In the appendices to the chapters, I also present simple game-theoretic analyses of some of the more important problems. The purpose of the game-theoretic analyses is to show how the arguments that I make in the different parts of the book relate to one another (all the game-theoretic models that are introduced in subsequent chapters build on the simple models that I introduce in Chapter 2). My game-theoretic modeling strategy has one thing in common with Tsebelis's models of veto-player interactions (2002): they deal with the strategic interaction between a *given* set of political decision-makers (the game-theoretic models that I examine in Chapters 3 and 5 do include elections, but the elections are treated as stochastic events, as in Besley and Persson 2011). But there is also an important difference between my approach and Tsebelis's. In Tsebelis's work, the basic modeling construct is a model of a two-dimensional policy space in which political parties and institutional veto players take different positions. Since I wish to concentrate on the specific problems of compensation and reforms, my argument requires a different approach. My basic modeling construct is therefore more closely related to the types of games that are examined in the international-relations literature on political bargaining and armed conflict (see, for example, Fearon 1995).

In the empirical sections, I discuss a wide range of examples drawn from comparative studies of policymaking and reforms. My main goals are to develop a comprehensive theoretical argument, to test some of the implications of that argument, and to illustrate the main points of the argument with the help of empirical examples. I do not test each of the propositions that can be derived from the theory. In some cases, I present new evidence. In other cases, I rely on earlier empirical studies (by myself or others). In some cases, I present theoretical propositions that have not yet been tested.

I combine evidence from large-$N$ studies of political decision-making (especially from Europe and the English-speaking former settler colonies in North America and the Asia-Pacific region, but also from Latin America) with case studies of political systems and events that provide especially interesting examples of conflicts over reform. The policy areas that feature most prominently in the book are trade policy, labor market policy, fiscal policy, social policy, tax policy, and macroeconomic policy. Interestingly, the connections between compensation, side payments, and the ability of political decision-makers to adopt and implement policy reforms have often been examined in more detail in the applied literature on particular policy areas than in the general literature on political institutions and decision-making.

I avoid lengthy discussions of research design and methods, referring readers who are interested in these problems to the articles and papers that the empirical sections are based on.

There is one methodological choice that I would like to discuss in some detail, however. Since I define reform capacity as the highest level of conflict that a political system can tolerate before reforms cease to be adopted, the outcome of interest in all of the empirical examples that I discuss is *policy decisions*. As I mentioned earlier, it would be inappropriate, given the specific objectives of this book, to treat policy *outcomes* as the main *explanandum*, which is what makes my approach different from that of authors such as Roller (2005), Gerring and Thacker (2010), and Lijphart (1999, 2012).

But I am not interested in *any* policy decisions, since the argument that I am making is only concerned with the adoption, or nonadoption, of "reforms"—policies that are expected to have net benefits for society. We cannot treat *any* significant policy change relative to the status quo as a reform. It would also be inappropriate to treat "legislative success," the ability of the executive to win support for its policy initiatives in the legislature (Cheibub et al. 2004, 578), as the explanandum to be studied (it is entirely possible to have high reform capacity in systems where the executive enjoys little legislative success, as long as members of the *legislature* introduce bills that address pressing economic and social problems). I have therefore sought to identify policy areas where it can plausibly be argued that at least in some periods, political conflicts have been positive-sum. I argue for these choices on a case-by-case basis throughout the book.[13]

Scholars, politicians, and intellectuals have long disagreed on a fundamental question of democratic theory: how power and authority should be allocated among institutions and political parties in a well-functioning democracy. In this debate, political scientists often contrast two ideal-typical models of democratic government: on the one hand, systems that embody a majoritarian "vision" of democracy, that have few veto players, and that excel at one of the two main mechanisms of democratic control, accountability; on the other hand, systems that embody a proportional "vision," that have

---

[13] The relevance of the empirical examples that I discuss in the book depends on the sometimes controversial assumption that the political conflicts that I am studying were at least *perceived* as "positive-sum" (in the sense that political decision-makers agreed that something should be done but disagreed on how to do it). But it is not clear that other methods that have been used to separate reforms from what we might call "ordinary" policy changes are superior. One approach that is common in economics is to simply stipulate which policies are better and then measure the adoption of "good" policies. For example, Duval and Elmeskov (2005), in a widely cited paper, examine the "progress" that European countries have made in the areas of labor- and product-market regulation by scoring policy changes positively or negatively "depending on whether the measure considered is in line or at odds with the general thrust of OECD policy recommendations" (Duval and Elmeskov 2005, 15). Many political scientists, by contrast, have sought to get around this problem by stipulating, on the basis of newspaper coverage, what the political "agenda" in a country is. For example, Mayhew (1991) identifies what he calls "innovative" policies with the help of both contemporary political commentary (the editorial pages of the *New York Times* and the *Washington Post*) and secondary literature. Binder (1999) argues, similarly, that political "gridlock" occurs when the political system fails to respond to problems that are on the "systemic agenda," which is a set of problems that the "political community" perceives as important. Empirically, Binder uses a content analysis of unsigned editorials in the *New York Times* to determine what the agenda is, the argument being that "the nation's paper of record responds to issues under consideration in Washington and highlights public problems that deserve attention" (Binder 1999, 523).

many veto players, and that excel at "representation" (on accountability and representation, see Przeworski et al. 1999). I call the first type of system "power-concentrating" and the second "power-sharing." The choice between these two types of democratic system is typically described as a trade-off: either you get effective governments with strong accountability mechanisms (lacking in inclusion and representation) or you get inclusive, representative governments (lacking in effectiveness and accountability); you cannot have both.

I don't think that this is the choice we are facing. The idea that we must give up inclusive government to get effective government seriously underestimates the ability of political decision-makers to overcome democratic paralysis by compensating losers.

# 2

# Compensating the Losers

In Chapter 1, I argued that the problem of reform capacity can be solved in two different ways. The first solution is to build political institutions that make it possible for governments to *ignore* losers (those who are harmed by a reform). The second solution is to build political institutions that make it possible for governments to *compensate* losers. Political decision-makers in power-concentration systems can, if they wish, rely on the first solution. Political decision-makers in power-sharing systems often rely on the second solution, since the first solution is more rarely available to them.

This chapter develops the book's central argument about political institutions, compensation, and reform. I begin by analyzing the term "compensation," as well as related terms such as "side payments" and "logrolling." I then show how compensation facilitates policy reforms in power-sharing systems. Following the discussion of these conceptual and theoretical problems, I demonstrate empirically that compensation has in fact been used to bring about important policy reforms. In the final section, I explain how the in-depth analyses that follow in subsequent chapters build on the arguments in this chapter.

The claims that I make here are not specific to any particular place and time. I therefore present empirical evidence from different parts of the world, and from different periods. The first of my two main examples is international trade policy. Political parties, interest groups, and economists have debated the benefits of free trade and protectionism for centuries, so for this part of the empirical analysis, it makes sense to include a large number of countries and to cover a long period. I therefore examine evidence from Europe, the Asia-Pacific region, and the Americas, and I begin more than a century ago, in the year 1900. My second example is labor market policy. I concentrate on reforms that are designed to push the unemployed to seek, find, and accept jobs. This political issue has only been salient in the advanced industrialized democracies for a few decades. It therefore makes more sense to concentrate on a smaller number of countries and a shorter period.

## Compensation and Side Payments

The ordinary meaning of the term "compensation" is "[a]mends or recompense for loss or damage" (*Oxford English Dictionary*). We compensate those who have been harmed by giving them something, or doing something for them, to make up for their loss. In this book, the term compensation has a more specific meaning: it refers to a public policy that is adopted to provide benefits for individuals, groups, parties, or organizations that have been (or expect to be) harmed by another policy.

A "side payment"—in bargaining theory, theories of international negotiations, and game theory—is a payment that is made to induce a decision-maker to support an agreement. In some contexts, side payments are understood to be monetary transfers; in other contexts, side payments can be either monetary or nonmonetary. Either way, the purpose of side payments is to render decision-makers that would otherwise be uncooperative cooperative. The concepts of compensation and side payment are not coextensive: in politics, winners do not always compensate losers to make them support new policies, and those who receive side payments have not always been harmed. But the two concepts are often used interchangeably, and I use them interchangeably in this book.[1]

The term side payment is not meant to suggest that the payment happens outside of the regular political process ("on the side"). On the contrary, I only examine side payments that have their basis in legislation or other authoritative political decisions.

In legislative bargaining, side payments often result in "logrolling," "vote trading between legislators" (McLean and McMillan 2015).[2] Some authors distinguish between logrolling and compensation since logrolling means that both parties to a bargain change their positions, whereas compensation means that only one party changes its position (and is compensated for this concession by the other party) (Pruitt 1981, 153). But the two concepts have a lot in common, and as Pruitt points out, logrolling can be defined as "mutual compensation."

---

[1] The reason that the terms compensation and side payments can be used interchangeably in this book is that political decision-makers are assumed to be rational and motivated only by the interests of the groups that their parties represent. This assumption implies that political agents only compensate losers when they need to secure support for policies that would otherwise not be adopted (no compensation without side payments). It also implies that political agents only block reforms that would actually harm them, so side payments are not required to build support for reforms that do not harm anyone (no side payments without compensation).

[2] McLean and McMillan (2015) add that the purpose of such vote-trading is commonly understood to be "to obtain legislation or appropriations favourable to the legislator's home district, with the understanding that 'you scratch my back, I'll scratch yours.'" The reason is that the term originated in the United States, a political system where individual politicians are highly responsive to local interests.

Logrolling is often seen as a questionable practice (as is the related practice of "pork-barrel politics"). As I discussed in Chapter 1, however, it is important to distinguish between what is politically expedient and what is ethically desirable, and logrolling is one of the political techniques that can be used to build support for major policy changes in power-sharing systems. Evans (1994) shows, for example, that pork-barrel projects have often been used to build support for general-purpose legislation in the United States Congress. As Cox and McCubbins (2001, 62–3) put it, distributive policies are "the currency that pays the cost of producing policy in polities that feature many and diverse veto groups"; without logrolling "policy making in these multiactor systems would be much more difficult and, probably, much more rare."

In the international-relations literature on bargaining among states, the term that is typically used to refer to mutual policy concessions is "issue linkage" (Tollison and Willett 1979). By "linking" policy domains, negotiators are able to aggregate seemingly nonnegotiable issues into "one package that is mutually beneficial for both parties" (Hopmann 1996, 81–2). The international-relations term issue linkage thus refers to the same types of bargaining mechanisms that I explore in domestic politics.[3]

We can think of compensation, side payments, logrolling, and issue linkage as different forms of political *compromises*. A compromise, in everyday language, is a "partial surrender of one's position, for the sake of coming to terms" (*Oxford English Dictionary*). In their book *The Spirit of Compromise*, Amy Gutmann and Dennis Thompson (2012, 10) define a *political* compromise more precisely as "an agreement in which all sides sacrifice something in order to improve on the status quo from their perspective, and in which the sacrifices are at least partly determined by the other sides' will."

To keep things simple, I stick to the terms compensation and side payments, which refer directly to the political strategies that I examine in the book.

The idea that compensation and side payments are important phenomena in politics is not new. As I discuss in more detail elsewhere in this book, there is a large applied literature on the role of compensation and side payments in specific policy areas, such as international trade. There is also a long-standing theoretical literature about these phenomena in political science. For example, William H. Riker's classic *Theory of Political Coalitions* (1962) devotes a whole chapter to the problem of side payments. He observes that in politics, side payments take the form of "promises on policy," and he notes that such promises need not involve the policy that is currently under consideration, since political decision-makers can also make "promises

---

[3] Lax and Sebenius 1986, 218–19 discuss these sorts of mechanisms in more general terms.

about subsequent decisions" (Riker 1962, 108–14). I will come back to these important observations in Chapter 3.

What we still do not understand well is when compensation and side payments can be used, and are in fact used, to build support for reforms. Abstract models of political decision-making typically assume either that side payments are always possible (as in the literature on cooperative game theory) or that they are never possible (as in Tsebelis's theory of veto players). But things are rarely that simple. Compensation is possible sometimes, but not always. "Parliamentary deadlocks occur when logrolling is impracticable," Thomas Schelling writes in his brilliant "Essay on Bargaining" (1956, 290). Yes, but when *is* logrolling impracticable? That is one of the questions that I will try to answer in this book.

In practice, compensation can take many different forms in politics: targeted tax cuts, subsidies, and transfers are just a few of the alternatives that are available. I provide numerous examples in the empirical sections of this book. As I will show, the policy that is used to compensate losers can, at times, be far removed from the policy change that the losers are being compensated for (as I discuss in Chapter 3, choosing a policy that is further removed is advantageous since it helps to reduce the "dilution costs" of compensation).

Sometimes political parties and interest organizations seek compensation for themselves, not for their supporters or members. One recent empirical study of this phenomenon is Davidsson and Emmenegger's (2013) analysis of the role that trade unions have played in Western European employment protection reforms. Davidsson and Emmenegger find that in many cases, trade unions have defended their own organizational interests more actively than the economic and social interests of their members. These two types of interests are not necessarily contradictory—parties and interest organizations may want to protect their organizational interests since they wish to maintain their ability to further the long-term interests of groups they represent—but they can be. The question whether parties and organizations are true agents of the groups that they represent is not of crucial importance for my theoretical argument—compensation can be used to facilitate reforms either way—but the answer to this question is likely to tell us a great deal about why reforms have different distributional effects in different countries.

This brings me to a related point: sometimes the *harm* that a political party suffers as the result of a reform is itself political, in the sense that the adoption of a reform does damage to the party's future political prospects. For example, Fernández-Albertos and Lapuente (2011) develop a model in which opposition parties have incentives to block policies that they in fact approve of since they have electoral incentives to prevent the government from claiming credit for popular reforms. In theory, it should be straightforward to compensate political parties for the harm that they suffer as a result of popular reforms: the winners just need to provide the losers with some other advantage, political or policy-related. But political gains and losses complicate political decision-making. They increase the total volume of compensation that needs to be provided, which, as I discuss in Chapter 3, increases the economic and political costs of compensation. More importantly, political gains and losses may create difficult-to-solve intertemporal commitment problems: the winners may become so strong, politically, that they end up having no incentive to honor the promises that they have made to the losers.

## Power Sharing, Compensation, Reform

This book compares two ideal-typical political systems: systems with power-concentrating institutions (where a single party controls the executive and the executive does not have to negotiate with other parties before adopting new legislation) and systems with power-sharing institutions (where several parties must come to an agreement before new policies are adopted).

There are several different types of power sharing. Power can be shared, first of all, within the executive. Coalition government, which means that the government consists of several parties rather than a single party, is a very common form of power sharing. In the parliamentary democracies in Western Europe, coalition government has been the most frequent type of government since the Second World War (Müller and Strøm 2003, 2). Coalition governments are also common in presidential systems. In the large sample of countries that Cheibub et al. (2004) analyze, in periods when the president's party did not control a majority of the legislative seats, approximately 50 percent of all governments in presidential systems have been coalition governments.

Coalition government is the type of power sharing that I will pay the most attention to in this book's empirical sections. The basic constitutional choice that I have the most to say about is therefore the choice between majoritarian and proportional elections (coalition governments are much more common in proportional systems than in majoritarian ones).

Power can also be shared between the executive and the legislature. This can happen in presidential systems if the president's party is not the majority party in the legislature (a type of situation that is called "divided government" in the United States). But it can also happen in parliamentary systems if the party, or parties, that are included in the government do not control a majority of the seats in the legislature (minority government). Either way, the executive cannot take for granted that its budget and its legislative initiatives will be adopted by the legislature, creating the need for political bargaining between the party, or parties, that control the executive and the party, or parties, that control the legislature.[4]

Power can also be shared within the legislature. This is commonplace in multiparty systems (especially in countries with proportional representation, in which it is rare for a single party to win more than half of the legislative seats), in bicameral systems (when the two chambers of the legislature are controlled by different political parties), and in systems with procedural rules that empower the minority party (as in the United States Senate, where the "filibuster" rule has long made it possible for a minority of senators to block important decisions).

Finally, power can be shared between the central government and regional, or state, governments. That is how federal systems work (at least if the policy competencies of national and regional governments are not so sharply delineated that the two levels of governments never need to coordinate their policies).

I will come back to the differences between these forms of power sharing in Chapter 3. For now, I will concentrate on what they have in common, which is that political power is divided, requiring agreement between political parties (or, in the case of federalism, between the national government and regional governments) before new policies are adopted. That is not the case in an ideal-typical power-concentration system, in which the power to adopt new policies is concentrated in a single political party that controls both the executive and the legislature.

Reforms that do not make anyone worse off are likely to be adopted in both power-concentration systems and power-sharing systems.[5] But most reforms harm some people, and those losers are more likely to be politically influential in power-sharing systems than in power-concentration systems. If it is not possible to compensate the losers, reforms that make some people worse off are therefore more likely to be adopted in power-concentration systems than in power-sharing systems. That is why the concentration-of-power hypothesis suggests that governments can only be strong enough to overcome conflicts over reform in power-concentration systems.[6]

---

[4] Laver and Shepsle (1991) discuss the basic similarity between divided government and minority government. On minority governments in parliamentary systems, see Strøm (1990).

[5] This leaves aside the possibility that reforms may be delayed by waiting games if different political parties prefer different versions of the same type of reform, as in the model developed in Alesina and Drazen (1991). I return to the possibility of delays when I discuss "urgent" political problems (situations in which delays are very costly) in Chapter 5.

[6] The concentration-of-power hypothesis assumes that it is straightforward for political parties in power-concentration systems to resolve conflicts between factions within parties. The large political parties that compete for power in power-concentration systems are themselves combinations of factions (Bawn and Rosenbluth 2006), so although a ruling party in a power-concentration system can typically impose its will on others, it still needs to deal with the problem of how to reconcile different ideas and opinions *within the party itself*. I will assume for the sake

26

But this argument excludes the possibility of compensation (combining a reform with other policy changes that provide benefits for those who expect to be harmed). By definition, a reform is beneficial for society as a whole. This means that reforms generate a "surplus," and it should in principle be possible to redistribute some of that surplus from the winners to the losers, making everyone better off.

For an example of a reform that involved compensation for losers, consider the major labor market reform that was adopted by the Danish parliament, *Folketinget*, in 1994. Preceded by years of negotiations between Denmark's trade union confederation and employers' association, this reform was a clear example of a policy package that included compensation for losers: the trade unions, and their political allies, the Social Democrats, agreed to cut the duration of unemployment benefits—harming some of their own supporters—but only in return for large investments in active labor market training programs. Without this compensation mechanism, the reform would not have been possible (Torfing 1999; see also Lindvall 2010a, Chapter 4).

Governments in the small, rich democracies in Western Europe have been using social policies to compensate losers from trade and structural economic change for many decades, at least since the interwar period (Katzenstein 1985). But compensation, as a political strategy, is not only used in small Western European democracies. Consider the labor market reform that was adopted in Argentina in 1994, the same year as the Danish labor market reform that I have just described. For years, Carlos Menem's government had sought to reform labor law, but all its reform attempts had been blocked by the Peronist party and killed in a Congressional committee that was controlled by delegates loyal to Argentina's trade unions. In 1994, however, the government negotiated with the main trade union confederation, *Confederación General del Trabajo de la República Argentina* (CGT), putting together a policy package that later won support in Congress: the unions agreed to reform employment-contract legislation and reduce severance pay for certain categories of workers; in return, the government subsidized the union-run health system. Again, reform was possible once the supporters of reform (the "winners") provided the opponents (the "losers") with compensation, although it was a very different sort of compensation mechanism than the one that was set up in Denmark in the same year (Etchemendy 2001, 9–10).

Strategies of compensation are not only used in power-sharing systems. In his book *Crisis and Compensation*, Calder (1988) shows, for instance, that governments in Japan—which was dominated for much of the postwar period by

---

of argument, however, that political parties have effective internal decision-making procedures that allow them to reach policy decisions decisively and quickly.

a single political party, the Liberal Democratic Party—have frequently used a strategy of compensation to secure the continued dominant position of the ruling party. Supported by the business community, Liberal-Democratic governments introduced new welfare-policy initiatives in times of economic insecurity to diminish fears and uncertainties that might otherwise have led to declining support for the dominant party and the regime. The difference between power-sharing systems and power-concentration systems such as postwar Japan's is that for governments in power-sharing systems, compensation is often a necessity; for governments in power-concentration systems, it is optional—it is a strategy that the government can use at will, for its own political purposes.

It is more difficult to use compensation mechanisms to build support for reforms if political parties have very different preferences. Imagine a policy package that is designed to bring down government debt by increasing taxes and reducing spending. If political parties have similar political preferences over taxation and spending, it is easy to reach a compromise. If political parties have very different preferences, however, their initial proposals will be far apart, which means that they will have to adjust their positions more to reach a viable political compromise. One clear example of how ideological polarization complicates reform is the United States, where the ideological distance between Democratic and Republican members of Congress has been increasing at least since the early 1980s. During Bill Clinton's and Barack Obama's Democratic administrations (in 1993–2001 and 2009–17), conflicts over fiscal policy with the Republican-controlled House of Representatives resulted in two government "shutdowns" (a refusal by Congress to fund government operations), both of which lasted more than two weeks, and in recurring disputes over the so-called "debt ceiling" (the maximum amount of national debt that Congress allows the United States Treasury to issue).

If political bargaining is not costly, it is in principle always possible for political parties to compromise over reforms, even in a polarized system. But as soon as we allow for the possibility that compromises may be costly, as I do in Chapter 3, polarization becomes a major impediment to reform, since compromises are more costly in a polarized system.

The implications of the argument that I have developed in this section are easy to understand. If compensation is possible—and if political decision-makers can solve the bargaining problems that I deal with in Chapter 3—reforms should be more or less equally likely to be adopted in power-concentration systems and power-sharing systems. But reforms will have different distributional consequences in these two types of systems. In power-concentration systems, the objections of losers from reform will often be ignored, which means that reforms are more likely to benefit some groups while harming others. In power-sharing systems, by contrast, the costs and benefits of reforms will be shared more evenly.[7]

## Reforming Trade

It is time to move from theoretical ideas to empirical evidence. In this section, and the following one, I show how governments have used public policies to compensate losers from reform. My first example, which draws on Brambor and Lindvall (2015), relies on data covering more than a century and concerns international trade policy. My second example, which draws on Knotz and Lindvall (2015), relies on data covering a thirty-year period and concerns labor market reforms.

The conflict between free trade and protectionism is a classic example of the type of political conflict between winners and losers that I examine in this book. It is generally accepted among economists that a policy of free trade increases national income (as Adam Smith and David Ricardo knew, there are "gains from trade"). But it is also generally accepted among scholars that some groups are harmed by free trade, and that if the "losers" are sufficiently powerful, they have both the means and the motive to block trade liberalization.

Unless the winners compensate the losers. The possibility of using the surplus generated by free trade to compensate the losers is described succinctly in Stolper and Samuelson (1941, 73), a famous paper on the distributional effects of free trade that ends by noting that "it is always possible to bribe the suffering factor by subsidy or other redistributive devices so as to leave all factors better off as a result of trade." If, when, and how governments can use compensation mechanisms to redistribute the gains from trade has been discussed in numerous theoretical and empirical studies in economics (Dixit and Norman 1986, Castro and Coen-Pirani 2003, and Davidson and Matusz 2006 are a few examples). There is also a long-standing literature on trade and compensation in political science. Scholars such as Cameron (1978) and Rodrik (1998) have demonstrated that there is a relationship between trade openness and the size of government, suggesting that governments use public spending to compensate losers from trade (see also Adserà and Boix 2002 and Hays et al. 2005), and Katzenstein (1985) has shown that

---

[7] An alternative way of studying compromise in politics is by examining an intertemporal, repeated game (see, for example, Dixit et al. 2000). What I do here is to study compromise in politics by allowing for side payments ("we'll assent to your proposal if you pay us"—see Roemer 2001, 8). I concentrate on side payments since I believe that compensation is an important but understudied real-world phenomenon.

governments in the smaller Western European democracies have long engaged in "domestic compensation," using economic and social policies to compensate wage-earners for the economic costs and heightened social risks that come with economic openness.

For workers in sectors of the economy that are adversely affected by free trade, the most obvious compensation mechanism (or "bribe," in Stolper and Samuelson's parlance) is unemployment insurance, which protects workers from the economic harm caused by trade liberalization.[8]

Brambor and Lindvall (2015) examine the relationship between social policy and tariffs over a period of more than one hundred years, matching data on average effective tariffs from Clemens and Williamson (2004) and Lampe and Sharp (2013) with data on the introduction and coverage of unemployment insurance in different countries.[9]

Panel (a) in Fig. 2.1, which is adapted from Brambor and Lindvall (2015), describes the mean level of average effective tariffs in thirty-one countries in Europe, North America, and the Asia-Pacific region between the beginning of the twentieth century and the late 2000s (excluding all periods in which countries did not have democratic institutions). The countries are divided into three groups on the basis of the structure of their unemployment insurance systems.[10]

Before the First World War, few countries had any form of unemployment insurance (France's system, introduced in 1905, was the world's first). Already in this period, however, we find that unemployment insurance was associated with lower average tariffs: during the first fifteen years of the twentieth century, tariffs remained relatively high in countries that had not yet introduced unemployment insurance, but fell, just before the First World War, in countries that had.

In the interwar years, the differences among countries without unemployment insurance, countries with low-coverage unemployment insurance, and countries with high-coverage unemployment insurance are particularly stark. Almost all countries responded to the Great Depression—the deep economic crisis that began in 1929 and deepened in 1931—by increasing tariffs, but

---

[8] On unemployment insurance as the most important compensation mechanism for losers from trade, see Mares (2004).

[9] Due to the lack of pre-1930s data on the structure and coverage of unemployment insurance systems, Brambor and Lindvall (2015) created a categorical indicator that separates countries *without* unemployment insurance, countries with *low-coverage* unemployment insurance (less than 50 percent of the labor force are covered), and countries with *high-coverage* unemployment insurance (at least 50 percent of the labor force are covered). The main sources are the United States Social Security Administration's *Social Security Programs throughout the World* series of publications, the *Social Citizenship Indicator Program* (Korpi and Palme 2008), Flora et al. 1983, and Scruggs and Allan 2006; for details, see Brambor and Lindvall 2015.

[10] Note that the composition of the three groups changes as more and more countries introduce unemployment insurance and as countries experience democratization or democratic breakdowns.

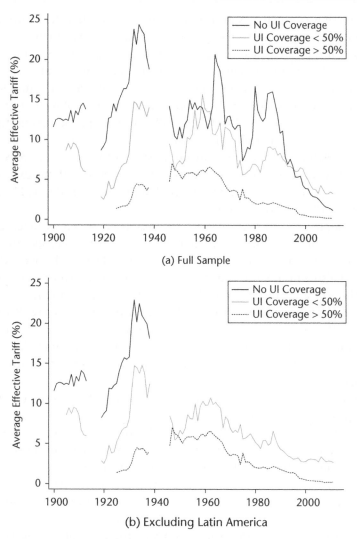

**Fig. 2.1** Unemployment insurance and tariffs since 1900.

*Comments*: The figure describes the relationship between the coverage of unemployment insurance (none, low, high) and the average effective level of import tariffs in a sample of thirty-one democracies since the year 1900, excluding the years 1914–18 and 1939–45 (the First World War and the Second World War). The countries included in the full sample are Argentina, Australia, Austria, Belgium, Bolivia, Brazil, Canada, Chile, Colombia, Costa Rica, Denmark, Ecuador, Finland, France, Germany, Greece, Italy, Japan, Mexico, the Netherlands, New Zealand, Norway, Peru, Portugal, Spain, Sweden, Switzerland, the United Kingdom, the United States, Uruguay, and Venezuela. Following Korpi and Palme (2008), Australia and New Zealand—which have unemployment insurance systems that are very different from those of the other countries in the sample—are coded as having low coverage.

*Source*: Adapted from Brambor and Lindvall (2015).

the increase was much less pronounced in countries that had introduced a comprehensive system of unemployment insurance. Meanwhile, countries that had introduced *some* form of unemployment insurance had lower tariffs than countries with no unemployment insurance system at all.

In the postwar period, countries without unemployment insurance continued to have higher tariffs than countries with unemployment insurance (by the end of the Second World War, all countries in the sample that had not yet adopted an unemployment insurance program were Latin American). The most distinctive group of countries in the postwar period were countries with high-coverage unemployment insurance systems: with the exception of the first few years after the Second World War, these countries had low tariffs throughout the postwar period.

The sample of countries that I have discussed so far is heterogenous: it includes not only the rich democracies in Western Europe and North America—which took part in the drive to free trade after the Second World War—but also a number of countries in Latin America, which pursued more protectionist trade policies, and which introduced unemployment insurance much later (Huber and Bogliaccini 2010). As panel (b) in Fig. 2.1 shows, however, the results are not driven by the regional differences between Latin America and the rest of the sample: panel (b) only includes Western Europe, North America, and Oceania, but nevertheless reveals a strong relationship between unemployment insurance and tariffs. The introduction of unemployment insurance—a policy that compensates losers from trade—does appear to make trade liberalization more likely, and more sustainable.[11]

The connection between trade liberalization and compensation was especially apparent in the early postwar period, when the postwar free-trade regime in the West began to emerge. As John Ruggie (1982, 396) observes, "the principles of multilateralism and tariff reductions" were complemented, in this period, with "safeguards, exemptions, exceptions, and restrictions...designed to protect...domestic social policies." One important event in the early post-war period was the creation of the European Economic Community, which later became the European Union and which led to the removal of trade barriers within Western Europe. Before the

---

[11] On the political underpinnings of the more recent shift to free trade in Latin America—which is associated with export-promoting supply-side policies and increased public employment rather than broad-based social spending—see especially Kurtz and Brooks (2008). The relationship between liberalization and compensation is not only noticeable in the area of trade. Mukherjee and Singer (2010) finds an interactive effect of International Monetary Fund stabilization programs and domestic policies when it comes to the implementation of capital-account-liberalization reforms, suggesting that a high level of welfare expenditures increases the credibility of promises of compensation in the context of liberalizing reforms. Brooks (2004) finds, similarly, that "compensation capacity," the ability to channel social benefits to the losers of financial liberalization, explains why some governments have liberalized capital accounts, when others have not.

Treaty of Rome was signed in 1957, the International Labour Organization (ILO) commissioned a group of economic experts headed by the Swedish economist Bertil Ohlin to examine the economic and social consequences of introducing free trade in Europe (ILO 1956). They concluded that there was no need for a common European social policy, but only because they expected that member states would compensate losers from trade on their own accord. As Kenner (2003) notes, it was generally assumed, at the time, that the interests of workers would be protected since European trade unions were strong and since Western European governments were already in the process of expanding social policies and strengthening labor regulations (Kenner 2003, 3).

The process of European integration provides many other examples of how compensation mechanisms have been used to build support for large reforms. Despite the move to majority voting rather than unanimity voting in some policy areas, the European Union remains a clear-cut example of a power-sharing system (Lijphart 2012, Chapter 2). As many scholars of the European Union and the European integration process have pointed out, compensation and issue linkage are two of the most important strategies that policymakers in the European Union have used to avoid democratic paralysis, which helps to explain one of the great puzzles of European integration: how a political structure that depends so much on cooperation can produce policy at all. Dyson and Sepos (2010, 3) note, for instance, that integration in Europe has often been facilitated by "buying off opposition," and Adrienne Héritier (1999, 16–17) argues that political decision-makers have often used a strategy of compensation to build support for major reforms.[12]

The clearest example of how compensation mechanisms have been used to build support for European integration is the introduction of the Single European Market in the middle of the 1980s. It was widely expected, at the time, that the countries that had the most to lose, economically, from the establishment of the Single Market were Greece, Ireland, Portugal, and Spain. One of the European Union's main redistributive programs, the regional funds, was created to compensate these countries for the losses that they were expected to suffer (Hix and Høyland 2011, Chapter 9).[13]

---

[12] Moravcsik (1999) suggests that the literature on European integration has sometimes over-estimated the importance of compensation and issue linkages, but he does conclude that these strategies have played a role. See also Tsebelis and Hahm (2014), which reaches a similar conclusion.

[13] The creation of the Common Agricultural Policy several decades earlier can also be seen as a way for West Germany to compensate France for German industry's increased access to French markets, and, more generally, as a way to compensate Western European farmers for the adverse effects of the modernization of the European economy after the Second World War (Milward 1992).

## Reforming Labor Markets

The section "Reforming Trade" showed that social policies have been used to compensate losers from trade ever since the interwar period, and perhaps even earlier. In this section, I discuss more recent political events.[14]

In the 1980s, the 1990s, and the 2000s, labor market reform was one of the most salient political issues in the rich democracies. After the deep economic downturns of the mid-1970s, early 1980s, and early 1990s, the rich democracies experienced long periods of high and persistent unemployment. According to an influential literature in labor economics, the persistence of mass unemployment was caused, at least in part, by ineffective labor market policies, including unemployment insurance programs that did not encourage the unemployed to look for new jobs. Although unemployment insurance as such does not necessarily increase structural unemployment, it seems essential to get the *design* of the unemployment benefit system right (Blanchard 2006, 45). In any event, that has been the premise of many of the labor market reforms that governments have introduced since the 1980s. Economists, international organizations, and many national governments have advocated the adoption of what Eichhorst et al. (2008) call "demanding" labor market reforms (see also Martin 2004, Dingeldey 2007, and Weishaupt 2011)—reforms that push the unemployed to look for, and accept, new jobs.

Most importantly, labor economists have long argued that an unlimited or very long duration of unemployment benefit entitlements increases the baseline level of unemployment, at least if unemployment benefits are not coupled with strong job-search requirements (Layard, Nickell, and Jackman 1991; Nickell and Layard 1999; Bassanini and Duval 2006; Fredriksson and Holmlund 2006). I therefore concentrate, in this section, on reforms that resulted in an effective reduction of unemployment benefit duration.

Governments in the 1980s, 1990s, and 2000s had strong incentives to introduce such demanding labor market reforms. There was not only a growing international consensus on their desirability. There was also a shift in the electoral landscape. Political scientists have long believed that welfare-state cutbacks are almost always unpopular and politically risky (Pierson 2001), but recent scholarship suggests that voters do not always defend existing social policies, especially if those policies are regarded as costly and inefficient (Cox 2001; Bonoli 2013; Davidsson and Emmenegger 2013; Giger and Nelson

---

[14] This section is derived in part from Knotz and Lindvall (2015), an article published in *Comparative Political Studies* on November 28, 2014 (DOI: 10.1177/0010414014556209).

2013). In particular, it appears that many voters have become less supportive of generous benefits for the unemployed, even in countries where support for the welfare state in general remains high, such as Sweden (Svallfors 2011).

But there are losers. Demanding reforms, such as cuts in unemployment benefit duration, are clearly harmful to those who are already unemployed, since the unemployed always have an interest in keeping long-term unemployment benefits in place. But they are also harmful to workers who face a significant risk of unemployment, at least if those workers expect that new good jobs will be hard to find. The rich democracies are undergoing a structural economic transformation: blue-collar industrial employment is declining and service-sector employment is increasing, and many workers who lose their jobs therefore face the prospect of having to accept lower paying jobs in the low-skilled service sector. Workers who face this risk have perfectly good reasons to hold on to long-term benefits, no matter what the labor economics literature says about the effects of long-lasting benefit entitlements on structural unemployment.

Since cuts in the duration of unemployment benefits have clearly identifiable losers, one might have expected that such reforms would be rare in countries with coalition governments (since coalition government is the most common form of power sharing). But that is not what has happened. Since the 1980s—when labor market reform became an important political issue in many countries—coalition governments have been just as likely as single-party governments to introduce labor market reforms that put more pressure on the unemployed to look for new jobs by reducing the duration of unemployment benefits: as Fig. 2.2 shows, the frequency of large unemployment benefit duration reforms was practically identical under coalition governments and single-party governments in a sample of thirty-one democracies in Europe, North America, and the Asia-Pacific region between 1980 and 2007.

The key difference between reforms adopted by coalition governments and reforms adopted by single-party governments, as Knotz and Lindvall (2015) show, was that coalition governments used compensation to build support for reforms. The most direct compensation mechanism that governments can use when benefit duration is reduced is to introduce or expand labor market training programs—increasing the likelihood that the unemployed will find new, good jobs before their unemployment benefits run out— and Knotz and Lindvall demonstrate that whereas coalition governments have combined demanding reforms with increased spending on labor market training, single-party governments have not, which strongly suggests that coalition governments have used spending on labor market training

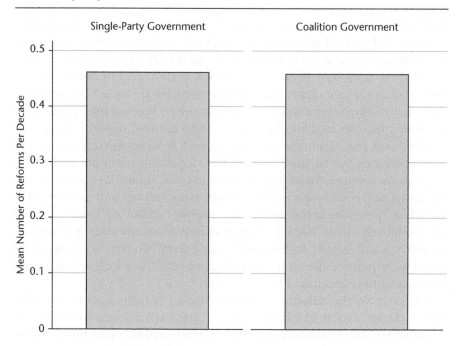

**Fig. 2.2** Unemployment benefit reforms, 1980–2007.

*Comments*: The figure describes the mean number of reforms that reduced the effective duration of unemployment benefits per decade, by type of government (coalition or single party). The following countries are included: Australia, Austria, Belgium, Bulgaria, Canada, the Czech Republic, Denmark, Estonia, Finland, France, Germany, Greece, Hungary, Ireland, Italy, Japan, Latvia, Lithuania, the Netherlands, New Zealand, Norway, Poland, Portugal, Romania, Slovakia, Slovenia, Spain, Sweden, Switzerland, the United Kingdom, and the United States. The analysis covers the years 1980–2007 (but the Central and Eastern European countries only enter the sample in the early 1990s).

*Source*: Based on data used in Knotz and Lindvall (2015).

programs to build support for reform instead of giving in to the opposition of potential losers.[15]

Fig. 2.3 describes this pattern, using data on public spending on labor market training from the OECD (the Organization for Economic Cooperation and Development). As the figure shows, the average level of spending on labor market training programs *increased* in countries where the effective duration of unemployment benefits was reduced if a coalition government was in

---

[15] Knotz and Lindvall's (2015) argument is related to that of Iversen and Soskice (2015), who provide a more general analysis of how electoral systems and party systems have influenced government responses to deindustrialization. For additional evidence of how compensation packages have been used in connection with labor market reforms, see the case studies in Castanheira et al. (2006).

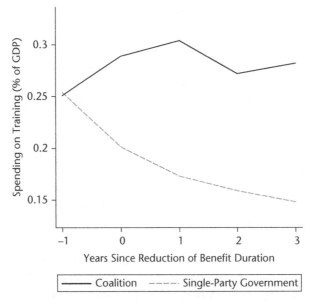

**Fig. 2.3** Unemployment benefit reforms and training.

*Comments*: The figure describes the average level of spending on active labor market training programs in countries where the effective duration of unemployment benefits was reduced, before and after such reforms (year of reform = 0), by type of government (coalition or single party).

*Source*: Adapted from Knotz and Lindvall (2015).

power, but *decreased* in the wake of such reforms if a single-party government was in power. This finding holds up in a statistical analysis that controls for a wide range of potential confounders (Knotz and Lindvall 2015, 598–603): the expected change in spending on labor market training programs is positive where duration reforms are introduced by coalition governments, but negative where such reforms are introduced by single-party governments.

Knotz and Lindvall's political explanation for this pattern is that coalition governments have stronger incentives to compensate groups that oppose demanding labor market reforms. Coalitions are made up of parties that need to proceed with caution when they introduce controversial reforms, whereas parties that are strong enough to form single-party governments are less responsive to demands from "losers" and more interested in appealing to a broader, more centrist electoral base. This explains why coalition governments have been more prone to use active labor market policies to compensate losers from labor market reform than single-party governments.

## The Pitfalls and Promises of Power Sharing

This chapter has discussed the meaning of the terms compensation and side payments, and it has shown that the possibility of side payments allows political decision-makers in power-sharing systems to overcome democratic paralysis by compensating losers. I have also discussed empirical examples of how political decision-makers have used compensation mechanisms to compensate losers from trade and losers from welfare-state reform.

But the analysis cannot stop there. The arguments that I have made so far have been highly abstract, and there are numerous practical problems and political complications that we need to take into account if we want to understand when it is possible to overcome conflicts over reform in power-sharing systems, and when it is not.

1. The analyses in this chapter have assumed that when a decision about compensation is made, that decision is implemented efficiently by the administrative agencies that are responsible for carrying out the government's policies. If the losers are concerned that the bureaucracy is inefficient, however, promises of compensation are worth less to them (see the section on deadweight costs in Chapter 3).

2. So far, I have assumed that there is always a side payment available, or, in other words, that political decision-makers always have a choice of policies that can be used to compensate losers. That is not always the case. Sometimes, important policy instruments are not available to national governments since they are controlled by regional governments or independent agencies. The government might therefore be forced to rely on other, less efficient instruments (see the sections on dilution costs and deadweight costs in Chapter 3).

3. Negotiating a policy package that includes compensation for losers can be politically costly. Political decision-makers need to devote time and other scarce political resources to such negotiations. They also need to consider the risk that their supporters, or potential supporters, will disapprove of the compromises they make. If these sorts of political costs are significant, reform capacity will be low (see the sections on internal costs and audience costs in Chapter 3).

4. Promises of compensation will be less valuable to losers if they fear that the policy used to compensate them will not be implemented faithfully. If the losers worry that other parties will use their influence over the bureaucracy to make sure that the losers are not compensated after all, reform capacity will be low (see the section on short-run commitment problems in Chapter 3).

5. The analyses in this chapter assume that compensation is instantaneous. In the real world, most political side payments are promises about future policies. It is rarely possible to determine *ex ante*, before a reform is implemented, who will in fact lose—and how much—and the harm that the losers suffer is often ongoing, not immediate. This means that promises about future policy have to be credible, and it is often difficult for political parties in democratic systems to make credible promises (see the section on long-run commitment problems in Chapter 3).

I will turn to all these problems in Chapter 3, in which I conclude that although compensation is possible *in principle*, it is often difficult *in practice*. But that is not the full story: power sharing can also have advantages.

6. So far, I have assumed that losers are only able to block reforms from within the political system. In many countries, however, the main obstacle to reform is not formal veto players, but interest groups that prevent governments from carrying out the policies that they have adopted. In Chapter 4, I show that in the presence of such "informal" veto players, power-sharing systems can have higher reform capacity than power-concentration systems.

7. My account of political decision-making in power-concentration systems has assumed, so far, that all the effects of reforms are instantaneous. But many reforms are costly in the short run and only become beneficial in the long run. We can call this category of reforms *investments*. Unless the governing party can "lock in" the policy that it adopts, it faces the risk that a future government might redistribute the benefits of the reform in a way that is harmful to the party that adopted the reform (turning that party into a net loser). In Chapter 5, I demonstrate that governments are more likely to undertake political investments in power-sharing systems.

The main implication of the arguments that I make in the rest of the book is that in the final analysis, the relationship between institutions and reform capacity depends on the relative importance of the weaknesses of power-sharing systems (points 1–5) and of power-concentration systems (points 6 and 7).

## Technical Appendix

In the appendices to Chapters 2–5, I present simple game-theoretic analyses of political decision-making in power-concentration and power-sharing systems. The game-theoretic models are stylized representations of the book's central arguments. Their main purpose is to identify the conceptual and theoretical connections between ideas that I discuss in different parts of the book. Specifically, the models make it easier to see how and why political conflicts play out differently under different sorts of institutions (Chapter 3), in different societies (Chapter 4), and in different policy areas (Chapter 5).

## The political system

In an ideal-typical power-concentration system, a single political party controls both the executive and the legislature, enabling that party to adopt any policy it wants without having to negotiate with other parties. In power-sharing systems, by contrast, two or more parties must agree on a policy change before it can be adopted, either because the cabinet consists of a coalition of parties or because the governing party does not control a majority of the seats in the legislature, or for both of those reasons (I am postponing the discussion of the special case of federalism until Chapter 3).

Consider, therefore, a political system in which two political parties, $A$ and $B$, compete for political influence. $A$ and $B$ represent two distinct social groups, with distinct political interests. We can think of one party as a left-wing party, representing low-income voters, and we can think of the other party as a right-wing party, representing high-income voters. Under power-sharing institutions, both $A$ and $B$ have veto power, in the sense that all policy changes, relative to the status quo, require the approval of both parties (Tsebelis 1995, 293). Under power-concentration institutions, by contrast, either $A$ or $B$ has veto power, and the other party does not.

The stylized political system that I have just described is the simplest possible theoretical representation of the differences between power-concentration and power-sharing systems. In any real society, there are more than two parties (and more than two relevant social groups), and political institutions are more complex. But keeping the analysis as simple as possible brings out the essential differences between different systems. We can think of the game-theoretic models as reduced-form games that correspond to more realistic political models.

To simplify matters further, I restrict the analysis to scenarios in which $A$ benefits more from a reform than the other party, $B$, and in which $A$ acts as the agenda setter ($A$ has the power to propose new policies, $B$ does not). The only difference between power-concentrating and power-sharing institutions is therefore whether $A$ is the *only* veto player, so that $A$'s proposals are adopted by default (power concentration) or whether $B$, the potential loser from reform, is *also* a veto player (power sharing).[16]

## Policy choices

The aim of the game-theoretic analyses is to describe the conditions under which political decision-makers adopt reforms, taking into account that reforms have different distributional effects.

The effects of reforms are described by two parameters that are known to both $A$ and $B$.

The net benefits of a particular reform are captured by the parameter $y \in (0, \infty]$, which is a benefit that both players receive if the reform is enacted, and which can be called the "welfare parameter," or, alternatively, the "efficiency parameter" (cf. Thomas Schelling's distinction between the "efficiency" aspect of bargaining and the "distributional" aspect of bargaining in Schelling 1956, 281 and George Tsebelis's distinction between "efficient" and "redistributive" institutions in Tsebelis 1990, Chapter 4). We can think of $y$ as the payoff that each player would get *if the benefits of a reform were distributed equally*.[17]

The distributional effects of a reform are described by the distribution parameter $\alpha \in [0, \infty]$. If a reform is enacted, $A$ receives a total payoff of $y + \alpha$ and $B$ receives a total payoff of $y - \alpha$. In other words, the parameter $\alpha$ describes how beneficial a reform is to $A$, relative to $B$. Using the two parameters $y$ and $\alpha$, it is possible to describe any type of reform: reforms that make both parties equally well off ($\alpha = 0$); reforms that make both parties

---

[16] On the relationship between proposal rights and veto rights, see McCarty (2000). In power-sharing scenarios, we can think of $A$ as the senior partner in a coalition government and of $B$ as the junior partner. Alternatively, we can think of $A$ as a single-party minority government and of $B$ as a party in parliament whose support $A$ needs, or of $A$ as the majority party in the lower house of a bicameral legislature, with $B$ commanding a majority in the upper house.

[17] The parameter $y$ can be seen as a measure of the aggregate benefit of adopting a new policy that is better adapted to current economic, social, and political circumstances than the existing policy. Following Acemoglu (2003, Section 2), let $Y$, which represents a proxy for aggregate social welfare (such as national income), be a function of $X$ and $P$ ($Y = F(X, P)$), where $X$ is a vector of economic and social conditions that cannot be altered by the government (at least not in the short run) and $P$ is a vector of policies that *can* be altered by the government. Still following Acemoglu (2003), define $\mathbb{P}(\cdot|X)$ as the set of policies that maximize $Y$, conditional on $X$. As Acemoglu observes, the set $\mathbb{P}$ may have more than one element—it is possible, even likely, that there are several different combinations of policies that could, if implemented, achieve optimal welfare—but if social welfare can be defined, there must be a nonempty set of policies that maximize it. If the status quo policy $P_{t-1}$ is not an element in $\mathbb{P}(\cdot|X_t)$, there is thus a nonempty set of potential policy *changes* that would increase $Y_t$ by replacing the status quo policy $P_{t-1}$ with a new policy, $P_t$. A reform is *welfare-optimal* if it replaces the status quo policy $P_{t-1}$ with a policy in the set $\mathbb{P}(\cdot|X_t)$. On this basis, we can define $y$, the parameter in the game-theoretic analyses, as

$$y = \frac{1}{2}(Y(P_t, X_t) - Y(P_{t-1}, X_t)).$$

better off, but make $A$ relatively better off than $B$ ($0 < \alpha < y$); reforms that make $A$ better off without making $B$ either better off or worse off ($\alpha = y$); and reforms that make $A$ better off and $B$ worse off ($\alpha > y$).

Following Alesina and Drazen (1991, 1176), we can think of $\alpha$ as a measure of the severity of political conflicts: a high $\alpha$ implies a high level of conflict between $A$ and $B$. More generally, we can think of $\alpha$ as a function of *two* factors: on the one hand, *overall* political polarization (for any given economic or social problem, political decision-makers in a more polarized system can be expected to propose solutions with more radical distributional outcomes); on the other hand, the nature of the *specific* economic or social problem that the reform is intended to solve (some problems require more radical measures than others).

I assume that $A$'s and $B$'s indirect utility functions $u_A$ and $u_B$ are linear, additive functions of $y$ and $\alpha$, so that $u_A = y + \alpha$ and $u_B = y - \alpha$ in the event of a reform and $u_A = u_B = 0$ in the event of no reform. In other words, the utility that both players derive from status quo policies is normalized to 0, and both players care equally about the magnitude of the policy effects described by $y$ and $\alpha$.[18]

Since the utility that both players derive from status quo policies is normalized to 0, the parameter $y$ can be taken to represent both the realization of positive improvements (such as the adoption of a new technology that allows the government to provide a public service more efficiently) and the avoidance of harms (such as the adoption of a fiscal consolidation program that lowers the costs of servicing the debt and reduces the risk of an economic downturn). Mathematically, these two effects are equivalent. We can thus use the same modeling framework to analyze both types of problems.

Unlike other models of reform, such as Fernandez and Rodrik (1991), the model that I am analyzing assumes that political agents have perfect information about the costs and benefits of reforms, about the distribution of those costs and benefits, and about each other's motivations. The justification for this simplifying assumption is that if anything, it should bias the results *against* my own theory. Note, for instance, that Fernandez and Rodrik's model suggests that when costs and benefits are uncertain, it is possible for a political system to be status quo biased even if the decision that individual voters face is an up-or-down vote on a particular reform (which means that there is no element of power sharing).[19]

---

[18] The model assumes, in other words, that the two parties treat the parameters $y$ and $\alpha$—and, later on, the compensation that losers from a reform are offered—as *comparable* in the sense that it is possible for the costs and benefits to offset one another. See the discussion of the "economic" and the "religious" view of politics in Chapter 1.

[19] There are models where uncertainty complicates negotiations over compensation (see, for instance, Mitchell and Moro 2006), so the effects of uncertainty are not clear-cut. On balance,

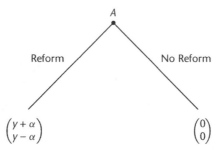

**Fig. 2.4** A power-concentration "game".

## *If compensation is not possible*

Let us begin by examining the relationship between institutions and political decision-making if compensation is *not* possible.

In a power-concentration system, $A$'s decision situation is straightforward (Fig. 2.4), since $A$ can simply do what it wants without taking $B$'s interests into account (indeed, one of the *points* of concentrating political power between elections is to make sure that the governing party does not need to worry about the objections of other parties until the next election). Since $y + \alpha$ is always greater than 0, $A$ always adopts a reform.

In a power-sharing system, the outcome does not only depend on $A$'s preferences, but also on $B$'s. Fig. 2.5 describes the simplest possible version of what we can call the power-sharing game, the power-sharing game without compensation. Here, once $A$ has proposed a policy, $B$ gets to either approve or reject that policy. The implications are clear. Since $y + \alpha > 0$, $A$ always proposes the reform. $B$ rejects the proposal if $\alpha \geq y$; otherwise, $B$ accepts (I assume throughout that $B$ only accepts a reform if $B$ benefits from it, not if $B$ is indifferent). In other words,

(a) if $\alpha < y$, $A$ proposes a reform and $B$ accepts it;
(b) if $\alpha \geq y$, $A$ proposes a reform and $B$ rejects it.

In a power-concentration system, then, the reform is always adopted, but in a power-sharing system, the reform is only adopted if $\alpha < y$ (that is, if the level of political conflict is low relative to the gains of reform). Under power-concentration institutions, only $A$ needs to be a winner. Under power-sharing institutions, both parties must be winners; otherwise, there will be no reform.

I have defined reform capacity as the highest level of conflict that a political system can tolerate before political decision-makers cease to adopt and

however, the assumption that the agents in the model have perfect information seems to bias the results in favor of the concentration-of-power hypothesis.

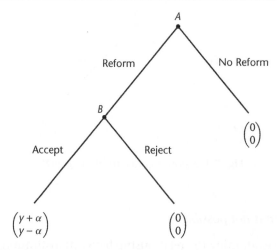

Fig. 2.5 A power-sharing game without compensation.

implement policy changes that benefit society as a whole (see Chapter 1). Let $\alpha^*$ be the maximum level of $\alpha$ that is compatible with reforms in equilibrium and let reform capacity, $R$, be the ratio between $\alpha^*$ and the total net benefit of a reform, which is $2y$. The ratio $R$ has a simple and intuitive interpretation: it represents the relationship between the *distributive impact* of a reform and the *total net gain* of a reform. If $R = 2$, for instance, reforms will be adopted if their total net gain is at least half of their distributive impact.

In the simple power-concentration scenario that I have considered in this section, $R$ is infinitely large ($R = \infty$): since $A$ does not need to worry about $B$'s losses at all, $A$ always has an incentive to adopt a reform, no matter how divisive conflicts are. In the power-sharing game without compensation, by contrast, $R = \frac{1}{2}$. Reforms are thus adopted for a much smaller range of parameter values in the power-sharing game without compensation. This is the simple intuition behind the idea that a concentration of power leads to more effective government.

### If compensation is possible

Now consider what happens when we introduce the possibility of compensation. Instead of choosing between two alternatives—proposing a reform or doing nothing—$A$ now chooses among *three*: proposing a unilateral reform (a reform with no compensation for the losers), doing nothing, or proposing a policy package that includes compensation.

Compensation can be modeled either as a *continuous* choice ($A$ is free to propose any level of compensation) or as a *binary* choice ($A$'s choice is

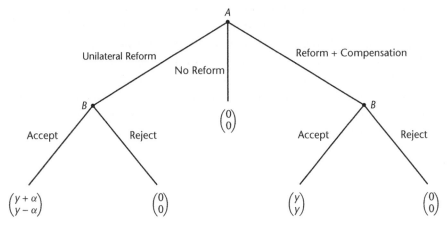

Fig. 2.6 A power-sharing game with compensation.

restricted to a particular level of compensation). Since allowing the level of compensation to vary would make some of the game-theoretic models that I discuss in Chapters 3–5 unnecessarily complicated, I will concentrate on a simple version of the power-sharing game, in which a strategy of compensation means that *all* the costs and benefits that are associated with a reform are shared equally between $A$ and $B$.

For now, I assume that compensation is costless. Later on, in Chapter 3, I will consider the possibility that compensation might be associated with economic and political costs.

In a power-concentration system, the possibility of compensation makes no difference, since $A$ never has any reason to compensate $B$. In a power-sharing system, by contrast, the possibility of compensation makes a big difference, ensuring (if compensation is costless) that reforms are always adopted in equilibrium. Fig. 2.6 describes the simplest possible version of the power-sharing game with compensation. If $B$ is a loser from reform ($y < \alpha$) or indifferent ($y = \alpha$), $A$ knows that $B$ will reject a unilateral reform, so $A$'s best choice is to propose a reform that includes compensation for losers (and $B$'s best choice is to accept, since both players prefer a reform that includes compensation for losers to no reform at all). If $B$ is a net winner ($\alpha < y$), $A$'s best choice is to propose a unilateral reform and $B$'s best choice is to accept. In other words,

(a) if $\alpha < y$, $A$ adopts a unilateral reform and $B$ accepts;

(b) if $\alpha \geq y$, $A$ adopts a reform that includes compensation for losers and $B$ accepts.

Either way, there is always reform in equilibrium.

If costless compensation is possible, the level of reform capacity does not vary between power-concentration and power-sharing systems: reform capacity is infinitely high ($R = \infty$) in both types of system, since the magnitude of $\alpha$ does not matter (distributional conflicts never lead to inaction).

But the distributional consequences of the reforms that are adopted vary: if $B$ is a loser from reform, $B$ can always get a better deal as a veto player in a power-sharing system than as a powerless opposition in a power-concentration system.

# 3

# How Reforms Fail

In the first two chapters, I argued that it is at least in principle possible for political decision-makers in power-sharing systems to overcome democratic paralysis by compensating losers from reform. I also showed, on the basis of comparative and historical evidence, that this is something that governments actually *do* (indeed, it is something that governments have done throughout the history of representative democracy).

But what is possible in principle is not always possible in practice. In this chapter, I show that political decision-makers need to solve two difficult problems when they build support for reforms by compensating losers. First of all, compensation can be economically and politically costly, and political decision-makers take the costs into account when they decide whether a reform is worth pursuing. Second, winners cannot always commit to compensation, which matters greatly to a political system's level of reform capacity since promises of compensation will ring hollow if the losers believe that those promises may not be fulfilled.

If the problem of costs and the problem of commitment cannot be solved, reform capacity is low in power-sharing systems: political conflicts soon lead to democratic paralysis. An analysis of these problems therefore helps to explain why side payments are not always possible (cf. Tsebelis 2002, 285) and, consequently, why some power-sharing systems are more effective than others (cf. Schmidt 2002, 149).

The first part of this chapter is concerned with the costs of compensation: dilution costs (when compensation compromises the objectives of a reform), deadweight costs (when compensation is costly to implement), internal costs (when bargaining over compensation requires the expenditure of time, energy, and other scarce resources), and audience costs (when decision-makers pay a political price for being seen to negotiate with their political opponents). I conclude that all these problems need to be taken seriously—especially when they occur simultaneously—but I also show that the costs of compensation are much lower in some political systems than others.

The second part of the chapter distinguishes between two different types of political commitment problems: short-run commitments (a promise of compensation always needs to be credible until the next election, or, more generally, as long as the distribution of political power does not change) and long-run commitments (a promise of compensation sometimes needs to be credible *after* a change in the distribution of political power). The second problem is more difficult to solve than the first. Political decision-makers have come up with many institutional solutions to short-run commitment problems, but it is always hard for politicians in democracies to make long-run commitments. Long-run commitment problems are therefore a major cause of low reform capacity in power-sharing systems (as I discuss in Chapter 5, however, power-concentration systems are vulnerable to *other* commitment problems, which can be equally deleterious).

In both parts of the chapter, the discussion moves back and forth between theoretical arguments and empirical examples. The empirical examples include a comparative case study of labor market reforms in Belgium and the Netherlands, a comparative analysis of government debt in parliamentary democracies, and a discussion of democratic paralysis in the United States since the 1980s.

## Dilution Costs and Deadweight Costs

So far, I have assumed that if reforms are beneficial for society, making most people better off, it must be possible for the winners to share some of the gains with the losers. By definition, a reform generates a "surplus," an aggregate gain, so it should in principle always be possible for the winners to make a side payment to the losers, making both groups better off.

If compensation is associated with significant economic or political costs, however, the fact that a reform generates aggregate gains no longer guarantees that everyone can be made better off: an agreement to compensate the losers can only resolve conflicts over reform if the costs of compensation are low enough to make a reform worthwhile. This section identifies four types of economic and political costs, and explains how political institutions and procedures influence those costs.

The first problem that political decision-makers in power-sharing systems need to solve when they try to overcome conflicts over reform is to find a policy that can be used to compensate the losers. Compensation in politics is almost always indirect: the losers, being harmed by one policy change, are compensated through another policy change that is beneficial to them. The mechanism is typically not "we'll assent to your proposal if you pay us"

(Roemer 2001, 8); the mechanism is "we'll assent to your proposal if you agree to adopt another policy that we like."

One thing that political decision-makers will want to avoid, when they search for policies that can be used to compensate losers, is to compromise the objectives of the reform itself. Imagine, for instance, a reform that is meant to encourage technological innovation and growth by removing barriers to entry in a certain industry. If the losers (the industry insiders) are compensated by letting them hold on to some of their old privileges, the effects of the reform will be weakened.[1] Or consider one of the examples that I discussed in Chapter 2: labor market reforms that are meant to increase employment by putting pressure on the unemployed to look for jobs. If the losers (the long-term unemployed) are compensated by making them eligible for other benefits, such as early retirement (Ebbinghaus 2006), the reform will not serve the purpose that it was intended to serve.

A form of compensation that compromises the objectives of the reform itself can be said to have *dilution costs*. To avoid this risk, political decision-makers often rely, when they compensate losers, on a policy that is removed from the policy that is being reformed in the first place. The second policy needs to "fit" the first policy—in the sense that benefits can be targeted to losers from reform—but it should be a *different* policy. This, I think, is what Silja Häusermann has in mind when she argues that a political system's reform capacity depends on the interaction between the number of veto players and "coalitional flexibility" (2010, Chapter 5). Coalitional flexibility, in Häusermann's theory, refers to the diversity of political interests, and, consequently, to the prospects of trading policy concessions in different areas to find combinations that satisfy different groups at the same time. "Where coalitional flexibility is high," Häusermann notes (2010, 92), "veto power can be overcome by political exchange."

Political decision will also want to avoid policy alternatives that require the creation of a costly bureaucracy or that are otherwise inefficient. Inherently costly forms of compensation have *deadweight costs*. Like dilution costs, deadweight costs reduce reform capacity. To put it simply, if it costs the government $ 1.2 billion to provide the losers with $ 1 billion in compensation, the extra "deadweight cost" of $ 0.2 billion can potentially offset the aggregate gains of the reform, which may lead political decision-makers to decide that the reform package as a whole is not worthwhile. This is the sort of cost that Rodrik (1994) had in mind when he proposed a so-called "political

---

[1] Krusell and Ríos-Rull (1996) examine the political economy of this type of reform. They point out that it would in theory be possible to build support for reforms by compensating losers, but they assume that such policy packages are rare. They end by noting, however, that the political economy of compensation is not well understood: this is "the key question that needs to be addressed in future research in order to understand the role of different political institutions" (325).

cost–benefit ratio" to measure the "costliness" of reforms for policymakers: Rodrik's political cost–benefit ratio is meant to capture the idea that "for any amount of increase in the size of the national pie, the more reshuffling of income that is required to achieve that increase the more costly is the change to policymakers," since compensating the losers typically requires "distortionary subsidies and taxes" (Rodrik 1994, 67–9).

Dilution costs and deadweight costs are conceptually different. Dilution costs render the reform *itself* less effective. Deadweight costs increase the cost of *compensation*. But there are important commonalities.

It is likely that all forms of compensation are associated with *some* dilution costs and deadweight costs.[2] The important question for our purposes, however, is if dilution and deadweight costs vary between political systems (which would help to explain why reform capacity is lower in some systems than in others).[3] My answer to that question is that reform capacity is higher in systems where political decision-makers have many different options to choose from when they select policies that can be used to compensate losers. When politicians have more room for maneuver, they are more likely to find at least one alternative that is not associated with high dilution costs or deadweight costs. It is therefore a good thing, from the point of view of reform capacity, if political decision-makers have authority over many different policies (and if their preferences over those policies cannot be collapsed into a single dimension).[4]

Scholars sometimes treat complexity—or "multidimensionality"—as a nuisance in politics, since it renders coalition-building indeterminate and makes political outcomes unpredictable. But complexity can be a good thing: in my view, it is a necessary but not sufficient condition of high reform

---

[2] Davidson and Matusz (2006) investigate different instruments that can be used to compensate losers from trade and reach the conclusion that although the costs vary greatly between programs, the most efficient forms of compensation are cheap relative to the gains from trade.

[3] According to the Kaldor–Hicks criterion, a policy change is only an improvement over the status quo if it is in *principle* possible to compensate the losers, so the fact that it may be *inherently* costly to compensate the losers does not count against power-sharing systems.

[4] The literature on the legislative institutions of the European Union, which is a political system where most important policy decisions require unanimity or qualified majorities, provides evidence for this view. König and Junge (2010) show, for instance, that when political decisions involve several different policy areas, allowing for trade-offs among policies, the likelihood of policy change is higher. Aksoy (2012) shows, similarly, that complicated policy decisions make legislators more likely to change positions, suggesting that legislators find it profitable to engage in "within-legislation logrolls" to "secure favorable legislative outcomes." Kardasheva (2013) also studies package deals in European Union legislation. In an empirical study of referendums in Switzerland, Hessami (2016) shows that when the number of subjects per proposition in a referendum increases, the share of yes-votes also increases (at least until the number of subjects becomes so large that voters cannot assess the impact of the policy changes that are being proposed). This suggests that package deals can be used to build coalitions in referendums, just as in legislative politics and international negotiations. Hessami also finds that voters supporting a package deal have more heterogenous political preferences than voters supporting less complex propositions.

capacity in power-sharing systems. Imagine, for a moment, a group of national-level decision-makers that are rummaging through a toolbox filled with policy instruments, searching for one that can be used to compensate losers from reform. If many of the tools that can potentially be used to compensate the losers are in some *other* toolbox—the regional-government toolbox, for instance—it will be more difficult for national-level politicians to find an appropriate tool: if all the new and fresh tools are in some other toolbox, political decision-makers at the national level must make do with old and worn tools (tools with high dilution costs or deadweight costs). Whenever policymaking competencies are allocated to different levels of government, or to different institutions, the number of policies that the national government controls is smaller than it would be if the national government had authority over all policies, which reduces reform capacity.

The most obvious example of a political institution that allocates poli-cymaking competencies to different levels of government is federalism. By definition, federal constitutions remove certain policies from the jurisdiction of the national government (Riker 1975, 101). This means that a government in a power-sharing, federal system faces a choice when it tries to build support for reforms: either it relies on policies that it controls itself (which means that it may have to choose forms of compensation that come with high dilution and deadweight costs) or it engages in a broader process of political nego-tiations that also includes regional governments, which is likely to increase *internal* costs and *audience* costs (to which I turn in the next section).

But federalism is not the only type of institution that can complicate polit-ical bargaining by reducing the national government's room for maneuver. The number of policies controlled by national governments is also reduced whenever policymaking competencies are delegated from the state to inter-national organizations such as the European Union. States often have good reasons to delegate authority to international organizations (see Milward 1992 and Moravcsik 1999 on the European Union), but one consequence of such delegation is that the national-level policy space shrinks, complicating policymaking at that level.

The number of policies controlled by national governments is also reduced whenever national governments delegate policy competencies to indepen-dent agencies (Jordana et al. 2011) and to other independent institutions, such as central banks (Cukierman 1992) or fiscal policy councils (Calmfors and Wren-Lewis 2011). Again, governments often have good reasons to delegate authority, but there is a downside: delegation limits the range of policies that the national government controls, complicating national-level policymaking.

Finally, the national government's authority is at least in question if pol-icymakers must consider the risk that a constitutional court—or a court of appeal that is entitled to judicial review, such as the United States Supreme Court—may declare laws and executive orders unconstitutional.[5] In systems where judicial appointments are politicized, such as the United States, we can think of the role of the courts in a way that is similar to how we might think about the role of a politicized bureaucracy (see the discussion in the section "Commitment Problems" in this chapter): as a factor that "bends" policy systematically in the direction of one party's preferred policy.[6] In systems where judicial appointments are less politicized, such as Germany and the European Union, we can think of judicial review as a factor that simply makes the political process more uncertain.

I have concentrated on the value of institutions that leave politicians with many different options, since having room for maneuver makes it more likely that political decision-makers will be able to avoid forms of compensation that come with high dilution costs or deadweight costs. Another institutional factor that helps to explain why governments have more room for maneuver in some systems than in others is the quality of the bureaucracy. If the bureaucracy is inefficient, or corrupt, or both, deadweight costs increase. Dahlström et al. (2013) investigate the relationship between bureaucratic quality and government policies in one of the areas that I investigated in Chapter 2: active labor market policy. Their analysis shows that the average level of spending on active labor market programs is systematically lower in countries where the quality of the bureaucracy is low. Governments appear to be unwilling to spend money on programs that require bureaucrats to make discretionary case-by-case decisions if the bureaucracy is incompetent, corrupt, or both. An unreliable bureaucracy thus leaves political decision-makers with fewer options.

## Internal Costs and Audience Costs

Assume that the problem that I discussed in the section "Dilution Costs and Deadweight Costs" has been solved: there is a policy, or combination of policies, that can be used to compensate losers without incurring high dilution costs or deadweight costs. The next problem that political decision-makers

---

[5] The United States Supreme Court cases that arose from challenges to the health-care reform commonly known as "Obamacare" in the 2010s (see especially *National Federation of Independent Business v. Sebelius*, 567 U.S.__(2012), Docket No. 11–393) is one example of how the process of judicial review may threaten to remove individual pieces from a large policy package, compromising the package as a whole.

[6] In the United States, judicial appointments are politicized and judges are motivated by political attitudes (Segal and Spaeth 2002). This means that the ideological composition of the courts is likely to reflect the medium-run balance of power between the main political parties, and, consequently, that the actions of the judiciary are fairly predictably favoring some parties over others (on the U.S. Supreme Court as a "national policymaker," see Dahl 1957).

must solve when they put together a policy package is to determine what, exactly, the package should contain: they need to agree on a specific mix of policies that is acceptable to all of the parties that share power. How high should unemployment benefits be to compensate losers from trade? What kinds of tax breaks should private companies get in return for being forced to invest in cleaner technologies? How should a fiscal consolidation package be structured to make sure that the burdens are shared equitably among political parties? Those are difficult political questions, and reaching an agreement will typically require the expenditure of time, energy, and other scarce resources. If these decision-making-related costs are too high, bargaining will fail, and democratic paralysis will ensue.

In political science, the costs of decision-making are often called *internal costs*, which is also the term that I use. Giovanni Sartori (1987, 216–17) writes, for instance, that all collective decisions "have *internal* costs," which are "the *costs of the process of deciding*" (emphasis in the original). The idea of internal costs goes back to James Buchanan and Gordon Tullock's *The Calculus of Consent* (1962, Chapter 8), in which the authors analyzed the "costs of decision-making" and observed that those costs are increasing in the number of decision-makers, "probably at an increasing rate" (106). This idea has many applications in economics and political science. For example, Dixit (1996) suggests that increasing the number of veto players tends to increase the transaction costs associated with political bargaining, and Cox and McCubbins (2001, 27) note that a large number of veto players makes it more difficult to "structure negotiations," and to ensure that each party "receives sufficient value to accept the deal."

The key question is why internal costs are higher in some power-sharing systems than in others. One attempt to answer this question is Markus Crepaz's distinction (1998, 64–5) between "competitive" and "collective" veto points. Crepaz argues that there are important differences between veto players operating through "separate institutions with mutual veto powers" (which, according to Crepaz, *does* lead to an increased risk of political deadlock) and veto players who "operate in the same body and whose members interact with each other on a face to face basis" (which Crepaz believes leads to "collective agency and shared responsibility," not deadlock). Crepaz's idea that face-to-face interactions change the way politicians think—promoting collective agency and shared responsibility—is not compatible with the stylized, rationalist approach to political decision-making that I take in this book, but a more narrow interpretation of Crepaz's argument, according to which frequent face-to-face interactions reduce the internal costs of bargaining, *is* compatible with my argument.

Tsebelis (2002, 88) argues that the distinction between competitive and collective veto points is imprecise. He points out, for instance, that it is not

*[handwritten margin note: "Mr. Window? writing for decision makers"]*

clear why the communication between two legislative chambers in a bicameral system (competitive veto points according to Crepaz) should be less "face
to face" than the communication between a parliamentary government and
a unicameral legislature (collective veto points according to Crepaz). This
is an important point. There is no reason to assume *a priori* that face-to-
face communication is impossible among what Tsebelis calls "institutional"
veto players. Think of Germany, with its Mediation Committee acting as an
intermediary between the *Bundestag* and the *Bundesrat* (Chapter 2 in Tsebelis
and Money 1997 contains an overview of such intermediary institutions in
bicameral legislatures).

But the fact that it is not possible to make a neat, binary distinction
between "competitive" and "collective" veto points does not mean that
Crepaz's intuition about the importance of face-to-face interaction has no
merit. In my view, there are strong reasons to believe that internal costs are
lower if political decision-makers interact frequently on a face-to-face basis.

First of all, political negotiations do not need to start from scratch.
They will always build on other ongoing negotiations, about other political issues. Justin Kirkland (2011) has shown that legislators develop
working relationships with each other and that they benefit from these
relationships when they seek to achieve legislative outcomes. Drawing on
the sociologist Mark Granovetter's idea of the "strength of weak ties" (1973),
Kirkland shows empirically that repeated interactions with legislators from
another party are positively associated with legislative success in the United
States House of Representatives and in state legislatures across the United
States. "A legislature with more bridging ties," Kirkland (2011, 897) concludes, "should be able to be more responsive to changes in the political world than a more balkanized chamber, even in the face of polarized
ideal points."

Second, the internal costs of political bargaining are likely to be lower if
political decision-makers are well informed about each other's motivations
and interests. If the winners do not know how much the losers stand to
lose, and if the losers do not know how much the winners are winning, it
takes longer to negotiate a policy package than if both the losses and the
gains can be estimated with a high level of certainty. Frequent interactions
make it more difficult for political decision-makers to hide their true motives
and intentions. "In longer-term relationships," Gutmann and Thompson
(2012, 170) argue in *The Politics of Compromise*, "legislators have a better
sense of their colleagues' intentions, their trustworthiness, and the political
constraints they are facing—and their colleagues know that they do." This
fact "enables all to make more confident judgments about when to compromise." Again, it seems reasonable to conclude that if political decision-
makers interact frequently, on a face-to-face basis, internal costs will be

significantly lower than if political decision-makers are more remote from each other.[7]

In the beginning of Chapter 2, I distinguished among (1) power sharing *within the executive* (coalition government), (2) power sharing *between the executive and the legislature* (divided government in presidential systems, minority government in parliamentary systems), (3) power sharing *within the legislature* (within and between chambers), and (4) power sharing *between the central government and regional, or state, governments* (federalism). The frequency of face-to-face interactions is highest when political decision-makers interact within one institution. On average, I therefore expect that internal costs will be low in negotiations within coalition governments (1) and within legislative chambers (3), slightly higher in negotiations between governments and legislatures (2) and between legislative chambers (3), and significantly higher in negotiations across levels of government (4).

There is one more type of cost that is left to discuss: the *audience costs* that decision-makers suffer if agents outside the political decision-making process—such as interest organizations and important groups of voters— react negatively to the deals that political decision-makers are striking.

In political science, the term "audience costs" was first used in the field of international relations, referring to costs that "arise from the action of domestic audiences concerned with whether the [country's] leadership is successful or unsuccessful at foreign policy" (Fearon 1994, 577), but I am using it here in the context of domestic politics, referring to the potential consequences of having groups that are not involved in the bargaining process witnessing the bargaining process itself (as opposed to the *outcome* of the bargaining process) (see Groseclose and McCarty 2001).

Audience costs are likely to be lower—and reform capacity is likely to be higher—in systems where political decision-makers can negotiate *in secret*. This may seem like a paradoxical argument to make, since we typically think of openness and transparency as virtues, not vices. But it is an argument that has been made before. If political decision-makers face "audience costs,"

---

[7] It is also likely that a *habit* of compensating losers reduces internal costs. In systems where past political conflicts over reform have been solved by compensating the losers, that type of solution is likely to be simpler to adopt and implement in order to solve present conflicts. Imagine, for instance, a society where past conflicts over economic modernization, industrialization, and international trade were solved through compensation—perhaps by setting up transfer programs that benefited losers from trade—and imagine that the same society now faces another great economic dislocation (such as the transition from a largely industrial economy to an economy where the service sector plays a much more important part). Some of the programs that were set up to handle the first transition are likely to also facilitate the second, and even if they do not, the historical experience of the first transition is likely to simplify the search for solutions to the second. This argument suggests that there may be a "virtuous circle" in societies where compensation is an important political mechanism—early investments in compensation-based solutions to democratic paralysis make it easier to implement such solutions in the future. I am grateful to Per Andersson for instructive discussions about this problem.

they become reluctant to reveal information and make arguments that they would have been happy to reveal and make in secret communications.[8] The importance of secrecy in political negotiations is emphasized by Warren and Mansbridge (2013) in their report to the American Political Science Association's task force on democracy in the United States (see also Naurin 2007). In nonpublic interactions, Warren and Mansbridge note (106), "opposing parties can share their perspectives freely and come to understand the perspectives of others." They conclude that "the empirical evidence on the deliberative benefits of closed-door interactions seems incontrovertible" (108).

The United States is an especially interesting example of how transparency complicates political bargaining. Committee meetings in the House of Representatives and the Senate were long held behind closed doors, but in the 1970s, procedural changes adopted by the House and the Senate opened committee meetings to the public and the press (Rieselbach 1994). There are strong indications that these procedural changes had detrimental effects on lawmaking, reducing the willingness of House members and senators to seek political compromises. Ehrenhalt (1982, 2178) (cited in Warren and Mansbridge 2013) argues that the new rules "made negotiation and political self-sacrifice infinitely more difficult" and Binder and Lee (2015, 253) argue that the "move toward greater transparency in congressional operations" has become a "double-edged sword," offering several examples of how transparency has undone negotiations over important policy decisions in Congress.

But the United States is not the only example. For an example from a different part of the world, consider Ecuador, which is, as Andrés Mejía Acosta (2009, 114, Chapter 1) notes, a "very difficult environment for the adoption of economic reforms" since it is "plagued with multiple actors and diverging interests." Mejía Acosta shows that despite these adverse conditions, presidents have been able to form what he calls "ghost coalitions" by offering individual legislators political benefits in return for their support for the president's major initiatives. These ghost coalitions were built in a "concealed" fashion, so secrecy was a key condition of reform: "cooperation was secured as long as partners systematically denied any form of cooperation" (117–18). Mejía Acosta shows that the adoption of an "ethics code" by Ecuador's Congress in 1998, banning vote-selling and punishing it with removal from

---

[8] In the second of the three presidential debates before the election of 2016, Hillary Clinton, the Democratic nominee, received critical questions about a speech that she had given in 2013, in which she said, "I mean, politics is like sausage being made. It is unsavory, and it always has been that way, but we usually end up where we need to be. But if everybody's watching... all of the back room discussions and the deals... then people get a little nervous, to say the least. So, you need both a public and a private position." (The source of the quote is Hillary Clinton's speech to the National Multi-Housing Council on April 24, 2013.) The argument that I am making implies that Clinton was right.

office, made the political system significantly less flexible by removing some of the mechanisms that facilitated legislative bargaining.

One conclusion that we can draw from these two examples is that having a system that allows for regular, secret deliberations among decision-makers—facilitating efficient decision-making—requires low levels of perceived corruption. The congressional reforms in the United States in the 1970s were a response to a series of political scandals that had reduced the public's confidence in political institutions (Rieselbach 1994, 57). So were the reforms in Ecuador in the 1990s. If citizens suspect that policymakers are corrupt, they have strong reasons to demand high levels of transparency, since the loss of decision-making efficiency is likely to be made up by the decrease in corrupt behavior. If citizens trust their political leaders, however, they have good reasons to give them a little privacy.

In many Western European democracies, the meetings of legislative committees are closed to the public and to the press (and, in some cases, to other members of parliament). The most recent comparative overview of parliamentary committees in Western Europe (Strøm 1998) shows that committee meetings are secret in Denmark, Finland, Iceland, Luxembourg, Norway, Sweden, and Switzerland.[9] All of the Nordic countries, which are often described as surprisingly reform-prone given that power is almost always shared among several parties (McGann and Latner 2013), fall into this category. In majoritarian political systems, by contrast, committees are either public (as in the United Kingdom's House of Commons) or semi-public (as in the French National Assembly), which is arguably a consequence of the fact that there is less need to build support for policy packages in these legislatures. Successful power-sharing democracies create opportunities for political decision-makers to conduct sensitive negotiations in private.

## Reforms in the Low Countries

Let us compare two neighboring European countries, Belgium and the Netherlands. A comparison between these two countries will bring together many of the themes that I have discussed in this chapter so far, illustrating how the costs of compensation influence reform capacity.

In the early 1980s, open unemployment peaked in Belgium and the Netherlands, reaching approximately 11 percent of the labor force in both countries (Fig. 3.1). Then the two countries diverged. By the 2000s, the Netherlands was regarded as one the best examples of successful labor market

---

[9] Judging from the information available on the websites of the parliaments of these countries, Strøm's coding is still correct.

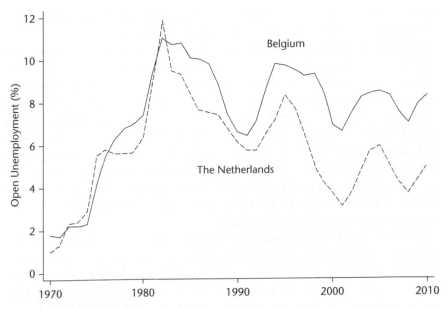

**Fig. 3.1** Unemployment in the Low Countries, 1970–2010.

*Comments*: The figure describes the level of unemployment—as a percentage of the civilian labor force—in Belgium and the Netherlands between 1970 and 2010.

*Data Source*: Armingeon et al. (2016).

reform in Europe (Viebrock and Clasen 2009). Meanwhile, unemployment remained high in Belgium, and a long series of OECD reports attributed this problem to the absence of comprehensive labor market reform, especially when it came to the nature of the unemployment benefit system. For example, even *after* the 2004 reform that I will discuss later in this section, the OECD's 2007 *Economic Survey* of Belgium called for more "efficient activation," pointing out that the unlimited duration of unemployment benefits is now an almost unique exception among OECD countries, and suggesting that the generosity of unemployment benefits should be reduced for long-term unemployed in order to encourage job search activity (OECD 2007, 66–71). For a long time, therefore, Belgium offered a clear example of a combination of policies that labor economists are particularly critical of: largely unconditional benefits with unlimited duration (Layard et al. 1994, 91–3).

The fact that Belgium and the Netherlands diverged in the 1980s, 1990s, and 2000s is puzzling, for these two countries are similar in many other ways (as their similar trajectories of unemployment in the 1970s also suggest). Politically, Belgium and the Netherlands are both dominated by the same three ideological traditions: Christian democracy, social democracy, and secular liberalism. Belgium has an additional, linguistic dimension in its party system—there are two social democratic parties (one French, one Flemish), two Christian democratic parties, and two liberal parties—but when it comes to the ideological composition of governments in recent decades, the similarities have been striking. Both countries had right-wing coalitions under Christian democratic prime ministers for most of the 1980s, but in the late 1980s, the Christian democrats Wilfried Martens (Belgium) and Ruud Lubbers (the Netherlands) reshuffled their cabinets, bringing in the social democrats (in 1988 in Belgium and 1989 in the Netherlands). These new coalitions lasted until 1994 (the Netherlands) and 1999 (Belgium), when they were replaced by "purple" coalitions between the social democrats and the liberals (with the social democratic leader Wim Kok as Prime Minister in the Netherlands and the Flemish liberal Guy Verhofstadt as Prime Minister in Belgium). The Dutch purple coalition lasted between 1994 and 2002; the Belgian lasted from 1999 to 2007. (Here, the similarities end, for in the Netherlands, Wim Kok's government was replaced by a new right-wing coalition, whereas Belgian governments after 2007 have been broader coalitions of left- and right-wing parties.)

The fact that the Netherlands was governed by ideologically mixed coalitions from the late 1980s to the early 2000s did not stop Dutch governments from adopting significant reforms. The reason was that governments were able to use side payments, making package deals that linked "demanding" activation measures (such as stronger job search requirements for the unemployed) to "enabling" measures (such as social protection for part-time workers and an expansion of active labor market programs). Although the liberal party *Volkspartij voor Vrijheid en Democratie* (VVD), a coalition partner in the 1994–2002 "purple" government, was skeptical about the effectiveness of labor market programs, they accepted the underlying compromise (Lindvall 2010a, 159). This compromise-oriented political style continued under the coalition between the liberal VVD and the Christian democratic *Christen-Democratisch Appèl* (CDA) that was formed after the "purple" governments. In 2006, the two Dutch unemployment benefit regimes were merged into a single new benefit, which had a maximum duration of three years and two months, unlike the previous benefit system, which had a maximum duration of five years. In return for this cut in duration, the replacement rate was increased from 70 to 75 percent in the first two months of unemployment (Sol et al. 2008). The reform was negotiated with the social democratic party. Again, the liberals had their reservations—in the parliamentary debate, representatives of the VVD stated that they had been opposed to the replacement-rate increase—but they accepted the package as a whole (Knotz and Lindvall 2015, 607).

In Belgium, by contrast, no large-scale labor market reforms were implemented in the 1980s and 1990s (or in the early 2000s). This was a period when Belgian governments only made minor policy adjustments (Van der Linden 1997, 290).

Since it is difficult to study the causes of nonevents, I will concentrate, in my discussion of Belgium, on the most important labor market policy change that *did* occur in the 1990s and 2000s: the 2004 "activation" reform, which was adopted under the liberal–social-democratic purple coalition that was in power in Belgium between 1999 and 2007. This reform did not change the basic parameters of the Belgian unemployment insurance system (benefits still have unlimited duration), but it did involve closer monitoring of the job-search behavior of the unemployed and new sanctions for unemployed individuals that do not actively seek work (Faniel 2005, 133–4).

Although this reform was relatively modest in comparison with unemployment benefit reforms elsewhere in Europe in the 1980s, 1990s, and 2000s, it came late, proved difficult for the government to adopt, and resulted in widespread social unrest across Belgium in the spring of 2004. The explanation, I argue, is that the distribution of labor market policy competencies in the Belgian federal system makes political bargaining much more complicated than in the Netherlands, where reforms could be worked out among the leading political parties, aided by negotiations with the leading interest organizations within corporatist institutions such as the Social and Economic Council (the *Sociaal Economische Raad*, or SER).

The distribution of labor market policy competencies between Belgium's national government and the autonomous regions of Flanders, Wallonia, and Brussels is complicated. The social security system, which includes unemployment insurance, is a federal matter. So is employment protection legislation (although labor law is also negotiated with the social partners). But the regions are responsible for active labor market programs. This means that there is a "fragmentation of competences" in labor market and social policy (Cantillon et al. 2006, 1035–6) (for an overview of the distribution of competencies in social and labor market policy in Belgium, see also de Deken 2007).

According to Frank Vandenbroucke, the federal minister who was responsible for introducing the labor market reform that was adopted in 2004, this distribution of competencies was an important part of the explanation for the fact that policies that were designed to encourage the unemployed to seek and accept new jobs came so late to Belgium. In a recent research report, Mr. Vandenbroucke, who has left politics, writes that the 2004 reform "was a second-best solution to the problem the Belgian labour market was struggling with since the 1980s: the institutional separation between, on the one hand, the control of the legality of unemployment benefits, which remained a federal competence, and, on the other hand, the assistance of jobseekers, which had become a regional power." Before 2004, Vandenbroucke and Lievens (2016, 19) note, "there was no effective communication between the 'punitive' and the 'helping' hand, causing *activation policy to be impossible*" (my emphasis).

This is a key point. Since the central level of government was responsible for the "demanding" (or "punitive") dimension of labor market policy, whereas the regional level of government was responsible for the "enabling" (or "helping") dimension, it was difficult to make trade-offs between demanding and enabling activation, as examined by Knotz and Lindvall (2015) and discussed in the previous chapter (see the Chapter 2 section "Reforming Labor Markets").[10] When the reform of 2004 was adopted, the federal government had to enter into a so-called "cooperation agreement" with the regional governments. This cumbersome political process began in December 2003 and complicated the development of a policy package that combined demanding and enabling activation measures. Although the responsible minister, Frank Vandenbroucke, presented the 2004 reform as a move toward a "Scandinavian" model, combining relatively strict conditionality requirements with programs that would help the unemployed to train for and find new jobs, the government was unable to include specific commitments to "positive" activation measures in its proposal—as minister, Mr. Vandenbroucke could only promise that he would initiate negotiations with regional governments concerning the *accompagnement* of the unemployed (Faniel 2005, 140). It seems safe to assume that a similar reform would have come sooner—and, perhaps, been more comprehensive—if it had been easier for Belgian coalitions to make package deals.

For Hemerijck and Schludi (2000) and Hemerijck et al. (2000), Belgium's low rate of social policy reform is associated with the conflict between the French- and Flemish-speaking communities (see also Béland and Lecours 2005, 277–81): the ongoing federalization process has undermined the "capacity for coordination and issue linkage at the national level," Hemerijck and Schludi argue, which means that reforms will only be possible if new "political and societal coalitions" can "reduce the plethora of veto powers in the Belgian political economy" (Hemerijck and Schludi 2000, 166). My interpretation is similar, although I have a different take on why those veto powers matter: in my view, the institutional fragmentation of political power

---

[10] Vandenbroucke et al. (2016) put the Belgian case in context by comparing it to other "multi-tier" polities, developing an argument about what they call "institutional moral hazard"—a situation in which two levels of government are involved in governing a social risk, and one level's actions affect the other level without that other level being able to monitor the situation. The argument is related to the argument that I am making here, but it is not directly concerned with the prospects for reforms, concentrating instead on the administrative level.

matters since it makes it difficult for political parties to construct broad policy packages.[11]

My conclusion is that if the policies that can be used to compensate losers are controlled by regional governments, national governments that wish to introduce reforms have a choice between two unappealing options. One option is to increase the number of veto players that must be accommodated in a package deal, through broad negotiations such as the "cooperation agreement" that preceded the Belgian labor market reform in 2004. But such a strategy typically increases both internal costs and audience costs—as the protests that followed the adoption of the Belgian reform plan in 2004 attest—and in some federal systems, it may not be possible at all. The other option is to make do with the policy instruments that national-level politicians control. But this strategy typically increases dilution costs and deadweight costs, again complicating the process of building support for reforms.

Like Belgium, the Netherlands is a power-sharing democracy, and the reforms that were adopted in the late 1980s and in the 1990s were introduced by ideologically diverse coalition governments. But the Netherlands is a different *kind* of power-sharing democracy than Belgium, and that makes a big difference.

## Commitment Problems

Let us assume that all of the problems that I discussed in the first part of the chapter have been solved: there are policies that can be used to compensate the losers effectively and efficiently (dilution costs and deadweight costs are low), political decision-makers agree on what the policy package should contain (internal costs are low), and they successfully avoid political exposure (audience costs are low). The next thing that political decision-makers need to worry about is implementation. Adopting policies is one thing, implementing them is another, and the losers know this. If the losers fear that they will not actually receive the compensation that they have been promised, they will typically block a reform even if it looks good on paper.

This would not be a problem if losers could be fully compensated right away when they support a reform. As I mentioned in Chapter 2, however, this almost never happens in politics. Except in rare cases, political side payments involve promises about *future* policy. It is rarely possible to determine *ex ante*,

---

[11] There are many other countries, apart from Belgium, where this logic should apply. Samuels (2003) shows that federalism complicates political coalition-building in Brazil: since legislators are typically locally oriented (concerned with electoral success at the state level) and since governors control resources that can be used to influence national legislators, presidents often need to negotiate with state governors when they build support for new legislation (81).

before a reform is implemented, who will in fact lose (or how much), and the harm that losers suffer is often continuous, requiring ongoing compensation. Consider losers from trade (which is one of the examples that I discussed in Chapter 2). When a trade reform is adopted, the risk that the losers face has not yet been realized (there are only *potential* losers from trade at that time), and there is no need for compensation until someone has actually been harmed. Moreover, the harm that the losers eventually suffer is not instantaneous, but ongoing (if you lose income each month because you lost your job or your wages fell, you want to be compensated each month).

As soon as the implementation of a policy of compensation comes after the reform itself, as it often does, there is an inherent commitment problem in any bargain between winners and losers. In other words, promises of compensation will only be credible if the winners are able to *commit* to compensating the losers: the losers need to be convinced that the winners will not use their political power to block compensation once the reform has been adopted and implemented. This is a difficult problem to solve, since agreements between political parties that control the state typically cannot be upheld by external authorities, such as courts, which makes political agreements very different from, say, contractual agreements between private companies (Acemoglu and Robinson 2001, 649–50). But reform capacity will be low, in power-sharing systems, if these problems cannot be solved satisfactorily.

We can distinguish between two types of commitment problems. A promise of compensation always needs to be credible in the *short run* (that is, as long as the current distribution of political power remains unchanged). If the losers cannot be fully compensated in the short run, a promise of compensation also needs to be credible in the *long run* (after a change in the distribution of political power).

I begin with the first problem, which is significantly easier to solve. In the short run, while the distribution of political power remains unchanged, promises of compensation lack credibility if the political parties that represent the "winners" are able to influence the implementation of the policy being used to compensate the losers. Imagine, for instance, a pension reform package that includes special provisions for blue-collar workers who started to work at a young age (this was, in fact, a contested issue in one of the French pension reforms that I discuss in Chapter 4). If the party that has appointed the minister of social affairs does not have the interests of those workers at heart, the minister of social affairs has an incentive to use his or her discretion to prevent the implementation of those provisions (say, by rejecting applications for early retirement). In these circumstances, the value of the side payment will be small for the party that represents the losers— smaller than it would have been if they were confident that the policy would be faithfully implemented.

These sorts of commitment problems are easier to solve in systems where the bureaucracy is more independent from elected politicians. The relationship between politicians and the bureaucracy varies greatly among democracies (Aberbach et al. 1981). In some countries, the bureaucracy is highly dependent on the political majority that controls the government, since bureaucrats are hired and fired on the basis of their political affiliations. In other countries, the bureaucracy is more independent from the executive, since bureaucrats are not political appointees. Reform capacity is likely to be lower in the first group of countries, since it is more difficult for the government to commit to implementing public policies faithfully if it controls the bureaucracy directly.

One solution to short-run commitment problems is therefore to reform the bureaucracy in a way that professionalizes the civil service and makes officials more independent from the executive. In such a system—which, as Moe and Caldwell (1994) observe, is more common under parliamentarianism—the problems described in this section are solved more easily. But that is not the only solution. Another solution, which is familiar from the literature on the political system of the United States, is to delegate authority to independent agencies outside the direct control of the executive in order to "lock in" the policies that the legislative majority has adopted. A third solution, which is familiar from the literature on corporatism in Western Europe, is to delegate authority to interest organizations through corporatist arrangements.

In addition to these attempts to solve long-run commitment problems at the *administrative* level, scholars of coalition government have studied solutions to short-run commitment problems at the level of political *decision-making*. There is a large literature on what partners in coalition governments can do to make sure that the decisions made within coalitions are faithfully implemented by ministries controlled by individual ministers representing different parties. Martin and Vanberg (2004, 2011) show, for instance, that coalition partners can use legislative committees as monitoring institutions to ensure that the policies that coalition governments have adopted are faithfully implemented. Other scholars, such as Timmermans and Moury (2006) and Strøm et al. (2010), emphasize other "coalition governance mechanisms" that can be used to manage such agency problems in coalitions.

Although the tried-and-tested solutions to short-run commitment problems may not be perfect—there is no way to completely avoid the risk of "implementation drift"—they go a long way. *Long-run* commitments, which extend beyond the duration of the current distribution of political power, are a more serious problem.

Long-term commitment problems are only a constraint on reform if the losers cannot be fully compensated in the short run. That is often the case, however. In the beginning of this section, I discussed the case of international trade, and I suggested that losers from trade typically cannot be compensated in the short run. The same could be said about the other example that I discussed in Chapter 2: labor market policy. A party that represents workers who risk losing their jobs will not agree to a demanding labor market reform such as a cut in unemployment benefit duration if they expect that the policy that is introduced to compensate the losers will only last until the next election. If the party that represents losers from reform is concerned that its political power will decline before the compensation scheme is fully implemented—and that future governments will not be bound by any promises that the "winners" made when the reform was adopted—then the losers will resist reform even if a combination of reform and compensation would in theory be to everyone's benefit.[12]

The difference between short- and long-run commitment problems is that it is more difficult to come up with institutional solutions to long-run problems. Most of the political solutions that I discussed in the context of short-run commitment problems, such as coalition governance mechanisms put in place to allow partners in multiparty governments to resolve commitment problems within coalitions, are inherently temporary: if the distribution of power changes, a new government can take back what the previous governments did. It is possible that some of the solutions that I discussed earlier can be made robust to changes in the distribution of political power. In the literature on the political system of the United States, for example, the delegation of authority to bureaucratic agencies is often seen as a way for political parties to "insulate" policies from future policy reversals (de Figueiredo Jr. 2002; see also Moe 1990). In general, however, it is very difficult for political decision-makers to prevent future decision-makers from changing policies and political arrangements.

This means that there is no easy fix for long-run commitment problems. They can only be solved if political decision-makers are either *unable* or *unwilling* to break promises to one another. There are strong reasons to believe, however, that this condition is often met in power-sharing systems.

First of all, large changes in the distribution of political power are more rare in power-sharing systems than they are in power-concentration systems. If political power is shared between several parties today, it is likely that power will also be shared among several parties tomorrow. Moreover, as Powell (2000) shows, opposition parties have more opportunities to influence the legislative process in proportional democracies than they have in power-concentrating majoritarian democracies, so even if the government is replaced by a different combination of parties, the political parties that

---

[12] We can think of this problem as a special case of the problem of "partial reform" that is discussed in Hellman (1998).

adopted a reform will typically have ways of making themselves heard in the future.

Second, parties only have incentives to break their promises to one another if they do not expect that they will depend on each other's collaboration and support in the future. A party representing "winners" will not break its promises to a party representing losers unless it expects that it will never again have to depend on that party in coalition formation or in parliamentary bargaining.

For these two reasons, long-run commitment problems are only likely to reduce reform capacity in power-sharing systems if the parties that represent losers from reform expect that they will experience a permanent decline in their political prospects in the near future. That can happen—particularly if a reform in *itself* is likely to harm the party's prospects in the future—but it is a special case, not the normal state of affairs in power-sharing democracies.

## Coalition Governments and Government Debt

The development of government debt is often used as an example of how and why power sharing leads to ineffective government. More than twenty-five years ago, in the 1980s, Roubini and Sachs claimed that "the size and persistence of budget deficits in the industrial countries... is greatest where there have been divided governments" (1989, 905–8). This idea has generated a vast literature in economics and political science, and the received wisdom has long been that there is a positive association between coalition government and increasing debt (see, for instance, Persson and Tabellini 2003, 179–83), although there have been many critics through the years (see especially Edin and Ohlsson 1991 and de Haan and Sturm 1997).

In this section, which is based on Bäck and Lindvall's analysis of the relationship between multiparty government and government debt (2015), I show how long-run commitment problems complicate reform in power-sharing systems, but I also show that commitment problems only affect a small proportion of all governments, since most governments appear to be able to solve those problems.[13]

The proposition that coalition governments tend to accumulate more debt than single-party governments can been derived from two different theoretical models. In "common-pool models," coalitions build up more debt since political parties (and/or individual ministers) externalize part of the costs of spending increases in the policy areas they care most about (Hallerberg

[13] This section is derived in part from Bäck and Lindvall (2015), an article published in *Political Science Research Methods* on August 4, 2014, which is available online at https://doi.org/10.1017/psrm.2014.11.

and von Hagen 1999; Hallerberg 2004): ministers from different parties have an interest in increasing the spending of their own departments even if the combined effect is to weaken the budget as a whole. Specifically, as Hallerberg and von Hagen (1999, 212) argue, if "each minister determines the spending priorities of her department, but...does not consider the full marginal tax burden," then multiparty governments are likely to accumulate more debt.

In "veto-player models," on the other hand, coalition governments accumulate more debt since they are less responsive to economic shocks than single-party governments are. As de Haan et al. (1999, 163) put it, "coalition governments will find it more difficult to close budget deficits after adverse shocks, since parties in the coalition will veto spending cuts or tax increases that impinge on the interests of their respective constituencies," resulting in what has been called "veto player deadlock" (Hallerberg and Basinger 1998; see also Alesina and Drazen 1991, Franzese 2002, Chapter 3, and Tsebelis 2002, Chapter 8).

The point that is made in Bäck and Lindvall (2015) is that these two models share a fundamental premise: they assume that factions within a majority party are better able to solve bargaining problems regarding fiscal policy than parties in a coalition are (as Persson et al. 2007, 2 put it, "a single-party government is assumed to behave as a unitary decision-maker, while a coalition government faces a collective choice problem"). Bäck and Lindvall argue that when coalitions have high "commitment potential"— that is, when they are able to solve long-run commitment problems since parties lack incentives to betray one another—there is in fact no practical difference between factions within a majority party and parties in a coalition government.

What, then, is commitment potential? Bäck and Lindvall's argument, which is closely related to the general argument about commitment problems that I discussed earlier, is that political parties fail to resolve long-run commitment problems in political bargaining when at least one party fears that its political power will diminish while other parties remain strong. The reason that factions within a party tend to behave like a unitary decision-maker whereas parties in coalition governments sometimes do not, Bäck and Lindvall suggest, is that parties in coalitions may have *outside options*—each member of a coalition government knows that there is some risk that its current partners will form other coalitions in the future (or govern alone). But that risk is much greater in some party systems than others. This is why commitment potential varies between coalition governments, and between political systems.

All fiscal policy decisions involve a basic trade-off. On the one hand, political parties have different preferences over taxation and spending, reflecting the distributional interests of the groups that they represent. On the other

*Commitment potential as horse or d.ssolution risk*

67

hand, political parties have reason to care about the fiscal and economic costs of high levels of government debt. Political parties are more likely to favor debt-reduction programs and other reforms made to achieve stable public finances if the adoption of such reforms does not cause great harm to their distributional interests. If political parties fear that if they lose power in the future, their current coalition partners will take the first available opportunity to change the distributional profile of fiscal policy in a way that harms them, they will be more likely to block all efforts to improve public finances, and debt will increase. But if parties are confident that their current coalition partners will not betray them in this manner, they will be just as likely to prioritize long-term fiscal goals as single-party governments are.

*[handwritten margin notes: debt reduction programs only if the distributional interests are not affected. Shake & balance of power]*

Building on this idea, Bäck and Lindvall develop an empirical measure of commitment potential that is based on historical patterns of cooperation among political parties in national party systems. They then use this new measure to show that coalition government is *only* associated with larger year-to-year increases in debt when the government's commitment potential is low.

Fig. 3.2, which illustrates this finding, describes the relationship between the average commitment potential of coalition governments and the average level of debt in 1960–2008 in advanced democracies where more than one-third of all governments were coalitions during this period. There is a strong cross-national correlation between the average commitment potential of coalition governments, on the one hand, and the average level of debt, on the other. Since this type of correlation might be the result of some third factor that influences both government formation and fiscal policy outcomes, Bäck and Lindvall (2015) estimate multivariate statistical models, which show that the relationship between commitment potential and the accumulation of government debt is robust to a range of checks and controls.

After the publication of Bäck and Lindvall (2015), David Weisstanner (2016) conducted a similar analysis of a larger sample of countries (thirty-six instead of the twenty that were included in the Bäck and Lindvall paper). Like Bäck and Lindvall, Weisstanner finds support for the hypothesis that commitment potential is an important factor that conditions the effect of coalition government on debt. He also finds support for a finding that was reported in Bäck and Lindvall (2015), but only received weak support in that paper: coalitions with very high levels of commitment potential appear to behave *more* responsibly than single-party governments. Weisstanner attributes this finding, plausibly, to the ability of strong coalition governments "to generate broad political support for controversial reform policies"—an argument closely related to the arguments that I make in Chapter 4 and Chapter 5 about situations in which power sharing leads to *higher* reform capacity than a concentration of power.

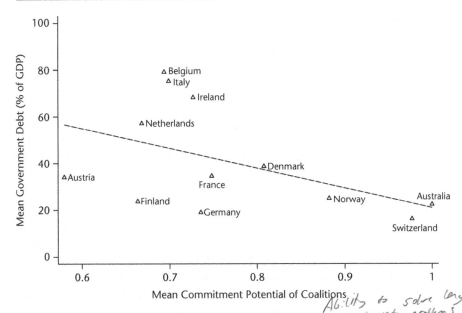

**Fig. 3.2** Commitment potential and government debt.

*Comments*: The figure plots the mean level of government debt in 1960–2008 (as a proportion of GDP) against the mean commitment potential of all coalition governments in advanced democracies where more than one-third of all governments were coalitions.

*Source*: Adapted from Bäck and Lindvall (2015). For definitions and data sources, see that paper.

*[handwritten margin notes: "Ability to solve long-run commitment problems is associated w/ lower gov. debt. • Long-term thinking (re institutional structure incentives that allow for longer..."]*

On the basis of these findings, there are strong reasons to conclude that the empirical relationship that has sometimes been observed between coalition government and the development of government debt in democracies is driven by a particular category of coalition governments: governments that are unable to solve the long-run commitment problems that I have discussed in this chapter.

## How Reforms Fail

This chapter has shown that political decision-makers in power-sharing systems need to solve two types of political problems if they wish to overcome democratic paralysis by putting together policy packages that include compensation for losers: they need to keep the costs of compensation low, and they need to solve the short-run and long-run commitment problems associated with political bargaining. If both the problem of costs and the problem of commitments can be solved satisfactorily, reform capacity will not be much lower in power-sharing systems than in power-concentration systems. Solving these problems is no easy task—but it is not impossible either.

Table 3.1 summarizes the main ideas and findings of this chapter. The problems that political decision-makers need to solve are in the left-hand column. The institutional and political conditions of high reform capacity in power-sharing systems are in the right-hand column.

The economic costs of compensation—dilution costs and deadweight costs—tend to be higher if political decision-makers have little room for maneuver when they search for policies that can be used to compensate losers. These costs also tend to be high if the bureaucracy is incompetent or corrupt (or both).

The political costs of compensation—internal costs and audience costs—tend to be high if political decision-makers do not interact frequently with each other, if a large number of decision-makers are involved in a decision, and if decision-makers are unable to negotiate in secret.

Commitment problems, finally, are more difficult to solve if the bureaucracy is politicized, if the parties that represent losers from reform are unable to monitor the implementation of policies being used to compensate losers, and if the parties that represent losers from reform worry that their political fortunes will decline in the near future.

The difficulty with the problems described in Table 3.1 is that they must be solved simultaneously, and the solution to one problem may compromise solutions to other problems.

The case study of labor market reforms in Belgium and the Netherlands discussed earlier showed that there can be a trade-off between dilution costs,

Table 3.1 Causes of reform failure in power-sharing systems

| Types of problems | Low reform capacity |
| --- | --- |
| Dilution and deadweight costs | Important policymaking competencies are divided between the national government and regional governments. |
| | Important policymaking competencies are delegated to independent agencies and/or international organizations. |
| | The bureaucracy is incompetent and/or corrupt. |
| Internal costs | Power is shared between different institutions (not between parties within one institution). |
| | The number of political decision-makers is large. |
| Audience costs | Political decision-makers have few opportunities to negotiate secretly. |
| Short-run commitments | The bureaucracy is politicized (and it is not possible to delegate administrative tasks to independent agencies, or to interest organizations). |
| | Coalition members and/or opposition parties are unable to monitor policy implementation. |
| Long-run commitments | The political parties that represent losers from reform expect that they will lose power before the losers are fully compensated. |

*power-sharing w/in levels, w/ strong commonur position),*
*A opaque, (untrans) power is most effectve*
*even in coalitions*

and deadweight costs on the one hand, and internal costs and audience costs on the other (since the policies that could be used to compensate losers effectively and efficiently were regional competencies in Belgium the government was forced to engage in a more complicated political bargain).

There can also be a trade-off between the problem of commitment and the problem of costs. One method of solving commitment problems, as we have seen, is to delegate authority to independent agencies, or to interest organizations, but this makes some policy options unavailable to future governments, which may lead to more severe problems with democratic paralysis down the line. In European democracies, corporatist structures that were created to facilitate postwar reconstruction and political coordination in the 1940s–60s became a source of gridlock and political stalemates in the period of economic crisis and austerity that began in the 1970s (see, for example, Hemerijck 1992 on the Dutch case). Scholars of politics in the United States such as Terry Moe (1990) and Rui de Figueiredo Jr. (2002) have shown, meanwhile, that political parties often create highly inefficient administrative arrangements when they seek to protect their favorite policies from future policy reversals by political opponents.

Another thing to note about the conditions of reform capacity summarized in Table 3.1 is that whereas some conditions of reform capacity in power-sharing systems are enduring features of the political system that political decision-makers cannot do much about in the short term, other conditions of reform capacity depend on political procedures and arrangements typically not codified in the constitution, which means that political decision-makers can, in principle, change those conditions.

To see this distinction more clearly, consider the implications of the ideas and findings in Table 3.1 for how to think about the causes of democratic paralysis in the world's oldest democracy, the United States. In the 1990s–2010s, reform capacity has been low in the United States. The clearest example is the recurring conflicts over fiscal policy that occurred during several of the periods of divided government in the 1990s–2010s. On many occasions during these years, the Republican majority in Congress threatened to block increases in government borrowing, in order to force the President to make concessions, and during both Bill Clinton's and Barack Obama's administrations, conflicts over fiscal policy resulted in "shutdowns" of the federal government.[14]

One plausible explanation for the democratic paralysis of the 1990s–2010s is increasing political polarization. As McCarty, Poole, and Rosenthal (2016) have shown, political polarization in Congress has increased dramatically

---

[14] Democratic paralysis is nothing new in the United States (see, for example, James MacGregor Burns's book *The Deadlock of Democracy*, which came out more than fifty years ago, in 1963).

in the United States in recent decades, pulling the two main parties, the Democrats and the Republicans, ever further apart.

But political polarization *in itself* does not lead to low reform capacity. I have defined reform capacity as the highest level of conflict (or polarization) that a political system can tolerate before reforms cease to be adopted. If this argument is correct, the nature of the political system in the United States must somehow make it difficult for political decision-makers to overcome polarization and resolve conflicts over reform.

The ideas and findings summarized in Table 3.1 suggest that the political system of the United States is, indeed, exceptionally vulnerable to democratic paralysis.

When it comes to the economic costs of compensation (dilution costs and deadweight costs), the combination of federalism, judicial review, and bureaucratic fragmentation makes it very difficult to adopt and implement comprehensive reform packages. The political costs of compensation—internal costs and audience costs—are also high. As I have shown in this chapter, the abolition of secret hearings in Congressional committees in the 1970s led to more adversarial relationships in the United States Congress. Meanwhile, the abolition of "earmarks" has made it more difficult to compensate losers, and the development of "campaigns without end" has compromised the policymaking process by forcing political decision-makers to put electoral needs above policy concerns (see Gutmann and Thompson 2012, Part 4). Finally, commitment problems are especially difficult to solve in the United States. When it comes to short-run commitment problems, the main constraint is that the United States has a more politicized bureaucracy than most other advanced democracies (Dahlström et al. 2012), and when it comes to long-run commitment problems, the system of separated powers in the United States tends to result in a separation of "purpose" between different institutions (Cox and McCubbins 2001), making commitment problems more difficult to resolve.

It is thus possible to explain the increasingly deadlocked nature of political decision-making in the United States with reference to three sets of factors. The first is polarization. The second is enduring features of the political system, such as federalism. The third is more recent procedural and institutional changes that have further complicated political bargaining and increased decision-making costs.

The fact that enduring institutional features do not explain everything is brought home by the fact that significant bipartisan reforms used to be more common in the United States. Consider, for instance, the political situation in the United States in the early 1980s. The 1980 elections in the United States resulted in divided government: the new President, Ronald Reagan, was a conservative Republican, and the Republican Party won a majority in the Senate, but the majority in the House of Representatives remained Democratic.[15] It was widely feared, at the time, that the ability of the political parties in the United States to block each other would prevent the federal government from responding to pressing national problems.

Contrary to expectations, however, the United States government was *not* unable to function after the elections of 1980. In 1983, two years into Ronald Reagan's first term, the Reagan Administration struck a deal with the majority party in the House, the Democrats, regarding a major reform of the national pension system: the Social Security Amendments of 1983 (Svahn and Ross 1983). The Democrats agreed to raise the retirement age and reduce cost-of-living adjustments. Meanwhile, Ronald Reagan agreed to increase payroll taxes (despite promises *not* to raise taxes) and to give up his opposition to Social Security, securing the long-term financial and political prospects of that program.

Even in the polarized political environment of the Reagan years, then, large-scale policy reform was thus possible in the United States. More recently, such bipartisan deals have been rare, and after the 2010 mid-term elections, many of the latent vulnerabilities and pathologies of power-sharing systems were laid bare. Divisive conflicts between the Democratic President and the Republican legislators in Congress in the early 2010s even prompted the American Political Science Association to form a task force to determine how to "negotiate agreement" in politics (Mansbridge and Martin 2013). The ideas and findings discussed in this chapter suggest, however, that democratic paralysis is not *only* an effect of enduring institutional features and increasing polarization (although polarization has indeed increased); there are feasible institutional reforms that could be introduced and that would increase the level of reform capacity in the United States.

This observation has important implications for the argument of this book as a whole. One important weakness of many institutional theories of political decision-making is that they cannot explain changes in political outcomes over time. The argument that I am developing in this book does not suffer from this weakness. My theory explains the outcomes of political decision-making processes with reference to the interaction between political institutions, political procedures (such as rules about secrecy and transparency in legislatures), the problems that policymakers try to solve, and the level of political conflict. It is therefore a theory that can explain why reform capacity varies within countries over time, even if overall institutional frameworks remain stable.

---

[15] This was when the word "gridlock" entered the political lexicon. Originally a "highway engineering term for a massive automobile traffic jam," gridlock was first used by a Chicago newspaper in late 1980 to describe a government "unable to function" as a result of party-political divisions (Safire 1993, 296; see also Binder 1999, 519).

The main implication of the arguments that I am making is that power-concentration systems and power-sharing systems are vulnerable to different "political pathologies." Democratic paralysis occurs for different reasons in different types of systems. In this chapter, I have examined the weaknesses of power-sharing systems. In Chapter 4 and Chapter 5, I will turn to the weaknesses of power-concentration systems.

## Technical Appendix

In the Technical Appendix to Chapter 2, I introduced a simple, game-theoretic framework that can be used to analyze political decision-making under power-concentration and power-sharing institutions. I defined the key outcome variable, reform capacity, as the ratio between the highest level of conflict that is compatible with the adoption of reforms in equilibrium, or $\alpha^*$, and the total net gain of a reform, which is $2y$. This ratio, $R$ (for reform capacity), represents the relationship between the *distributive impact* of a reform and the *total net gain* from reform. The higher $R$ is, the more conflict a political system can tolerate before it becomes impossible to overcome democratic paralysis.

In this Technical Appendix, I examine the consequences of the two types of political problems that I discuss in Chapter 3: on the one hand, the economic and political costs associated with compensation, and on the other hand, short-run and long-run commitment problems.

### If compensation is costly

The findings in Chapter 2 depend on the assumption that compensation is costless. As discussed at length in this chapter, that is not a realistic assumption, which is why many formal models of political bargaining assume that political side payments are, in fact, associated with costs (for two examples, see Castro and Coen-Pirani 2003, 1065, and Aghion et al. 2004, 577).

The simplest way to include the costs of compensation in the model is to introduce a cost parameter, $\kappa \in [0, \infty]$, which is a function of all of the four types of costs discussed in this chapter.[16] Consider, therefore, the power-sharing game with costly compensation (Fig. 3.3). The difference between this version of the power-sharing game and the version presented in

---

[16] $\kappa$ is increasing in dilution costs, deadweight costs, internal costs, and audience costs, but I am agnostic about whether these effects are additive or multiplicative (that is, whether, for instance, the internal costs are independent of the deadweight costs, or whether the internal costs themselves increase when the deadweight costs increase); most likely some of the effects are additive and others are multiplicative.

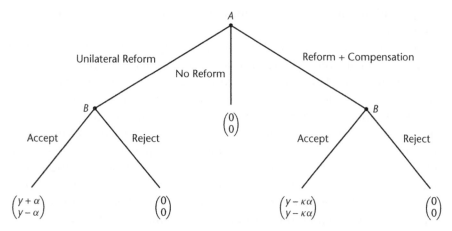

Fig. 3.3 A power-sharing game with costly compensation.

Chapter 2 (Fig. 2.6) is that in this game, compensation is (potentially) costly. The costs are assumed to be proportional to the volume of compensation, which means that a policy of compensation, if implemented, gives each player the total payoff $y - \kappa\alpha$ (each player's share of the gains from the reform, $y$, minus the costs of compensation, $\kappa\alpha$). If $\kappa = 0$, compensation is costless. If $\kappa > 0$, compensation is costly.

If $B$ is a net winner ($\alpha < y$), $A$'s best choice is, as before, to propose a unilateral reform (and $B$'s best choice, as before, is to accept). If $B$ is not a net winner ($y \leq \alpha$), $A$'s choice depends on the costs of compensation. If the costs of compensation ($\kappa\alpha$) are equal to or greater than the gains from reform ($y$), $A$'s best choice is to propose a unilateral reform, which $B$ will reject.[17] If the gains from reform ($y$) are greater than the costs of compensation ($\kappa\alpha$), on the other hand, $A$'s best choice is to propose a reform that includes compensation for the losers, and $B$'s best choice is to accept. In other words,

(a) if $\alpha < y$, $A$ adopts a unilateral reform and $B$ accepts;

(b) if $\frac{y}{\kappa} > \alpha \geq y$, $A$ adopts a reform that includes compensation for losers and $B$ accepts; and

(c) if $\alpha \geq \frac{y}{\kappa}$, $A$ adopts a unilateral reform and $B$ rejects it.

This means that $R = \frac{1}{2\kappa}$ if $\kappa \leq 1$ (otherwise $R = \frac{1}{2}$; from now on, when discussing games in which compensation is costly, I will assume that $\kappa \leq 1$). In other words, unless $\kappa \geq 1$, reform capacity is higher in the power-sharing game with costly compensation than in the power-sharing game without

---

[17] I am assuming, as before, that if $A$ knows that $B$ will reject any reform proposal, $A$ proposes a unilateral reform.

compensation, but there are circumstances in which there is no reform in equilibrium.

This result is illustrated in Fig. 3.4. As the figure shows, if the costs of compensation are very low, reforms are possible even if distributional conflicts are highly divisive, but as the costs of compensation increase, reform capacity declines. However, significant reforms are possible even if the costs of compensation are relatively high. Imagine a reform that increases national income by $ 1 billion (in other words, $y = 500$ million) and let us assume that transferring $ 1 from $A$ to $B$ in order to compensate $B$, the loser from reform, is associated with combined deadweight costs and political costs that are equivalent to 40 cents (in other words, $\kappa = 0.2$). Entering these numbers into the formula for $R$ reveals that even in this scenario, a reform will be adopted in equilibrium as long as $\alpha < 5$ billion. In other words, even when the total decision-making costs and deadweight losses associated with providing compensation correspond to as much as 40 percent of the actual compensation, reform is possible if the redistributive impact of the reform is less than 2.5 times the total beneficial effect of the reform.

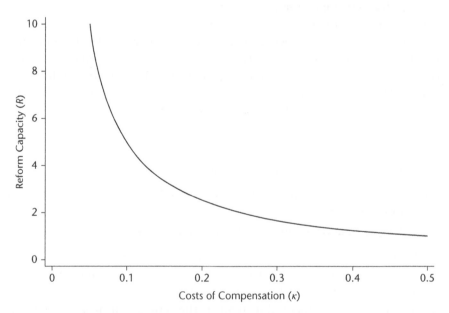

Fig. 3.4 Compensation costs and reform capacity.

*Comments*: The figure describes the implications of the solution to the power-sharing game with costly compensation (Fig. 3.3). For presentation purposes, the function is defined over the range $\kappa \in [0.05, 0.5]$. For even lower values of $\kappa$, $R$ approaches infinity.

## The bureaucracy game

In the section on commitment problems, I argued, among other things, that the independence of the bureaucracy matters greatly to reform capacity since an independent bureaucracy makes political decision-makers more confident that policy packages will be implemented faithfully. If the party that represents the winners is able to influence the bureaucracy, the party that represents the losers has reason to worry that the losers will not receive the compensation that they have been promised.

The bureaucracy game (Fig. 3.5) describes this type of situation. The difference between this game and the previous model is that there is now an extra "implementation stage" after the policymaking stage. After the adoption of a policy that includes compensation for the losers, $A$ chooses between using its influence over the bureaucracy (if any) to reduce the compensation that $B$ was promised and *not* using its influence in this way. $A$'s degree of influence over the bureaucracy is described by the parameter $\varphi \in [0, 1]$. If $\varphi = 0$, $A$ is not able to make the bureaucracy favor $A$'s interests at the implementation stage. If $\varphi = 1$, $A$ has complete control over the bureaucracy and is able to "bend" any policy as it pleases.

The bureaucracy game can be solved with backward induction. At the implementation stage—if $A$ has proposed a reform that includes compensation and $B$ has accepted it—$A$ always uses its influence over the bureaucracy

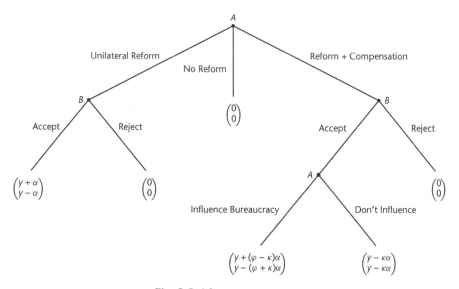

**Fig. 3.5** A bureaucracy game.

to bend policy in its favored direction (reducing the side payment). $B$ takes this into account when responding to $A$'s proposals. As in the power-sharing game with compensation, $B$ accepts a unilateral reform if $\alpha < y$; otherwise, $B$ rejects such a reform. If $A$ has proposed a reform that includes compensation, $B$ accepts the reform if $y - (\varphi + \kappa)\alpha > 0$; otherwise $B$ rejects the reform. Taking $B$'s strategy into account, $A$ proposes a unilateral reform if $B$ will accept it (or if $B$ will not accept a reform that includes compensation), and a reform that includes compensation if compensation is necessary and sufficient to win $B$'s support and makes $A$ better off relative to the status quo. In other words,

(a) if $\alpha < y$, $A$ proposes a unilateral reform and $B$ accepts;

(b) if $\alpha \geq y$ and $y - (\varphi + \kappa)\alpha > 0$, $A$ proposes a reform that includes compensation and $B$ accepts ($A$ then influences the bureaucracy as much as possible);

(c) if $y - (\varphi + \kappa)\alpha \leq 0$, $A$ proposes a unilateral reform and $B$ rejects it.

The level of reform capacity in this game is thus defined by

$$R = \frac{1}{2(\varphi + \kappa)}.$$

This result is illustrated in Fig. 3.6. In this figure, dark shades of gray represent high reform capacity and light shades of gray represent low reform capacity. As Fig. 3.6 reveals, reform capacity is high when low compensation costs are combined with a low level of politicization. Increasing the costs of either compensation or politicization (or both) results in lower reform capacity.

## The election game

I now turn to a game-theoretic representation of long-run commitment problems. Consider the political turnover game (Fig. 3.7), which is a simple model meant to capture the intuition that a high likelihood of political turnover may lead to long-run commitment problems.

Some time after the conclusion of an agreement between $A$ and $B$, elections are held, and with a certain probability, $A$ or $B$ loses power. If $A$ becomes the only veto player after the election, $A$ can—and will—stop implementing the policy being used to compensate $B$. The parameter $y \in [0, 1]$ describes the proportion of the compensation that is delivered after the election; $1 - y$ is consequently delivered before the election. If $y = 0$, the policy is fully implemented before the election. If $y = 1$, all of the compensation is meant to be implemented after the election.

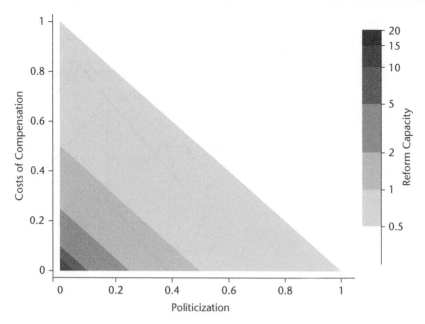

**Fig. 3.6** Politicization and reform capacity.

*Comments*: The figure describes the level of reform capacity (defined, here, by $\alpha^*$ divided by $2y$) as a function of the level of politicization of the bureaucracy (as defined by $\varphi$, $A$'s ability to bend policy implementation toward his favored policy, on the $x$-axis) and the costs of compensation ($\kappa$, on the $y$-axis). Dark shades of gray represent high reform capacity; light shades of gray represent low reform capacity.

The election game can be solved with backwards induction. If $A$ has proposed a reform that includes compensation, $B$ has accepted it, and $A$ wins the election, $A$ always reverses the policy (we are assuming, as before, that $A$ cannot credibly commit to not reversing a policy). Taking this into account, $B$ accepts a reform proposal that includes compensation if $q^A(y - y\alpha) + (1 - q^A)y - \kappa\alpha > 0$. Otherwise, $B$ rejects the reform. Taking $B$'s strategy into account, $A$ proposes a unilateral reform if $B$ will accept it, or if $B$ will not accept any reform, and a reform that includes compensation if compensation is necessary and sufficient to win $B$'s support *and* makes $A$ better off (relative to the status quo). In other words,

(a) if $\alpha < y$, $A$ proposes a unilateral reform and $B$ accepts;

(b) if $\alpha \geq y$ and $q^A(y + (y - \kappa)\alpha) + (1 - q^A)(y - \kappa\alpha) > 0$, $A$ proposes a reform that includes compensation and $B$ accepts;

(c) if $\alpha \geq y$ and $q^A(y + (y - \kappa)\alpha) + (1 - q^A)(y - \kappa\alpha) \leq 0$, $A$ proposes a unilateral reform and $B$ rejects.

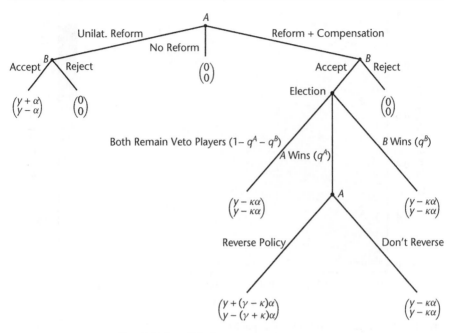

**Fig. 3.7** A political-turnover game.

The level of reform capacity in this game is thus defined by

$$R = \frac{1}{2(q^A \gamma + \kappa)}.$$

The implications of the analysis are easily seen in Fig. 3.8. As the figure shows, the level of reform capacity in this game depends on three factors: the costs of compensation, the likelihood that $A$ wins the election and governs alone, and the timing of the implementation of the compensation scheme. Reform capacity is highest when the costs of compensation are low, when the likelihood that $B$ remains a veto player is high, and when a large proportion of the compensation is implemented before the election.

This is a somewhat paradoxical result from the point of view of veto-player theory, for in this game, the expectation that the same parties that are veto players at time $t$ will also be veto players at time $t + 1$ makes reforms at $t$ *more* likely than otherwise. In other words, it may not be a disadvantage, from the point of view of reform capacity, to have more veto players, if all parties expect to keep their seat at the bargaining table in the future

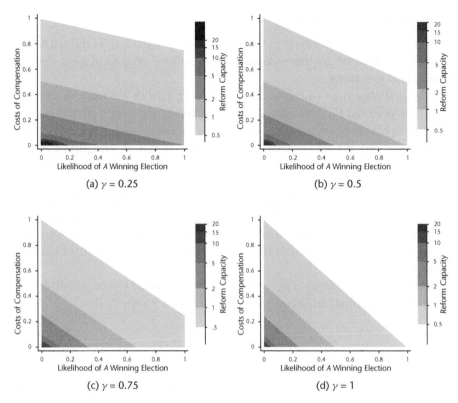

**Fig. 3.8** Political turnover and reform capacity.

*Comments*: Darker fields represent high reform capacity (the figure illustrates the results of the analysis of the political-turnover game graphically). The *x*-axis represents the likelihood that *B* will remain a veto player after the next election. The *y*-axis represents the costs of compensation ($\kappa$).

(cf. Lindvall 2010b). This observation is related to Callander and Krehbiel's idea (2014) that "supermajoritarianism" may impede change initially, but the promise of *future* supermajoritarianism helps to resolve intertemporal commitment problems: "Then, and with noteworthy irony, the same supermajority requirement that was the impediment to legislators' committing to the deal at the outset is essential to enforce the deal in the end" (825). The main conclusion, then, is that reform capacity is low in systems where there are many veto players today, but some of those veto players expect that they will not be veto players in the future.

## Measuring commitment potential

The measure of commitment potential developed in Bäck and Lindvall (2015) (which I discussed in the section on the politics of government debt) is calculated as follows.

The first step is to calculate each governing party's *potential for betrayal*, which is denoted $P_{i,j,t}$, for each country $i$, party $j$, and year $t$, on the basis of that party's history of participation in government. Since electorates, party systems, and political circumstances change, recent events provide more useful information about the manner in which parties behave than events far back in time. Bäck and Lindvall (2015) therefore let more recent years have greater weight by discounting past observations according to the discount rate $\delta$. We chose to set $\delta$ to 0.95, implying that events taking place some 14–15 years before the current observation—that is, approximately four electoral cycles earlier—have half the weight of events that took place the year before.

The formula for betrayal potential, which is inspired by the calculation of "democratic capital" in Persson and Tabellini (2009), is

$$P_{i,j,t} = (1-\delta) \sum_{\tau=0}^{\tau=t-t_0} \alpha_{i,j,t-\tau}\delta^{\tau},$$

where $\alpha_{i,j,t-\tau}$ is the proportion of party $j$'s coalition partners at time $t$ that were *not* in government with party $j$ at time $t-\tau$ (if party $j$ was in government at time $t-\tau$; if not, $\alpha_{i,j,t-\tau}$ is always 0), and $t_0$ is either 1945 or the first year of democracy (if democratization occurred later than 1945).

The reason that Bäck and Lindvall (2015) multiply the right-hand side of the equation by $1-\delta$ is that $P$ is thereby normalized to the interval $[0,1]$, where 0 means that the party has no history of governing without its current coalition partners and 1 means that the party has been in power continuously since the beginning of the period under observation without any of its current partners being included in previous governments.

The second step in the creation of the measure of commitment potential is to use each party's potential for betrayal, $P_{i,j,t}$, to calculate each *government's* commitment potential. Since no coalition government is stronger than its weakest link, Bäck and Lindvall (2015) define commitment potential as 1 minus the highest potential for betrayal of any of the parties in government at time $t$, so that

$$\text{Commitment Potential}_{i,t} = 1 - \max \mathbf{P}_{i,t},$$

where $\mathbf{P}_{i,t}$ denotes the set of "betrayal potentials" of the parties in government in country $i$ at time $t$.

Note that there are two ways for a party to acquire a high potential for betrayal. The first is when a party has recently been in government *together with a different set of coalition partners*. The other is when the party has recently *governed alone*. By definition, a party in a single-party government has a betrayal potential of 0, and a party has little or no potential for betrayal if it has exclusively, or almost exclusively, formed coalitions with the same partners prior to $t$ (or if it has never been in government at all).

# 4

# Formal and Informal Power

At this point in the book, the argument becomes more radical. So far, I have merely argued that power-sharing systems should fare *no worse*, when it comes to reform capacity, than power-concentration systems—at least if political decision-makers can handle the two problems that I discussed in Chapter 3, keeping the costs of compensation low and committing to policy packages that include compensation for losers.

In this chapter, and Chapter 5, I go further: I now argue that in some circumstances, power-sharing systems have *higher* reform capacity than power-concentration systems. I reach this conclusion by situating political institutions in space and time. The arguments that I have made in Chapters 2 and 3 have ignored two important facts: formal political institutions are situated in different kinds of societies ("space"), and the benefits of reforms are sometimes realized in the future, not in the present ("time"). I now consider the implications of these facts, beginning, in this chapter, with the first.

Most scholarly analyses of the relationship between political institutions and political decision-making are concerned exclusively with formal institutions, concentrating on the distribution of formal power within the political system and ignoring the distribution of informal power in society at large. But conflicts over public policy are often resolved in the street, or in lobbies, not in legislatures or government offices. Interest groups wield considerable political power—latent or manifest, sought or unsought—in modern societies. It is therefore important to examine and understand political conflicts between governments and interest groups. Formal institutions do not exist in isolation.

The main argument of this chapter is that the concentration-of-power hypothesis—the idea that reform capacity is higher under power-concentration institutions—only holds, if at all, in societies where interest groups have negligible informal power. Where interest groups have significant power, sharing power among several political parties may lead to higher reform capacity than concentrating power in a single party. I will show, more precisely, that reform capacity tends to be low if power-concentration institutions are situated in societies where interest groups are strong enough to threaten to block reforms, but not strong enough for the government to treat them as a permanent interlocutor.

This theoretical argument applies to all sorts of informal power—including the power of business groups, which is always great in market-based economic systems with private ownership (Lindblom 1977)—but the empirical sections of the chapter are concerned with one particular type of interest organization: trade unions. I concentrate on the case of trade unions for practical reasons. It is difficult to measure the informal power of other types of interest groups, such as business organizations, but there are widely accepted indicators of trade-union strength available (notably union density, the proportion of employed wage and salary earners that are members of trade unions).

The chapter's empirical sections present evidence that illustrates and supports my argument about the effects of institutions on political decision-making. I begin by using comparative data on labor market reforms in a sample of European Union member states to demonstrate that reforms are indeed adopted more rarely where formal power is concentrated, but civil society organizations are strong enough to threaten to block reforms. I then present a case study of pension reforms and labor market reforms in France, which is a country where many reform initiatives have been blocked by interest organizations. Finally, I use comparative evidence on political strikes to test another key implication of the chapter's theoretical argument: the proposition that political protests should be most common in power-concentration systems where interest groups have intermediate strength.

## Institutions and Interest Groups

The question for this chapter is how conflicts between governments and interest groups are resolved in power-concentration and power-sharing systems. Until now, the only form of power that I have considered is formal, or *de jure*, power, which is a form of power that is "allocated by political institutions (such as constitutions or electoral systems)"; I have not considered informal, or *de facto*, power, which "emerges from the ability to engage in collective action, or use brute force or other channels such as lobbying or bribery" (Robinson and Acemoglu 2006, 325–6). We can define informal power generally as the ability of interest groups to use "alternative political technologies" (Scartascini and Tommasi 2012), such as political protests, to prevent governments from carrying out the policies that they have adopted (either by blocking policy implementation outright or by causing so much disruption and unrest that the government is forced to back down; see Ellman and Wantchekon 2000, 502).

In the chapter's empirical sections, I concentrate on the political role of trade unions. The most important alternative political technology that trade unions have at their disposal is the *strike*, a form of protest that is "generally known and understood" in the modern world (Tarrow 1998, 98–100). Other interest groups seek political influence by other means, such as demonstrations, sit-ins, or other forms of protests.[1] The most important political technologies of business organizations, by contrast, are lobbying and, perhaps more importantly, the threat of causing direct economic harm by lowering investments or moving production to other countries (Lindblom 1977, 1982). Although I concentrate on trade unions, my general argument is relevant for all forms of informal power (but it only applies to interest groups that act strategically and instrumentally to influence policy).

Consider an interest group that has some measure of informal power, but no formal power (it is not represented by the political parties that control the government). If the government adopts a reform that harms this group, its rational response—assuming that the likelihood of success is sufficiently high and assuming that it is not too costly to use alternative political technologies—is to use its informal power to try to prevent the government from carrying out its policies. The question is what the government's rational response to this strategy is. Will the government offer the interest group compensation, to avert the threat? Or will the government risk a confrontation with the interest group by adopting a "unilateral" reform? Or will the government refrain from adopting reforms altogether?

The core of the argument that I wish to advance is that it is a more complicated affair to compensate interest groups than it is to compensate political parties. This is why reform capacity is sometimes higher in power-sharing systems (where key interest groups are more likely to be represented by at least one of the parties that control the government) than in power-concentration systems (where key interest groups more often lack access to formal political institutions).

First of all, unlike formal veto players, which are always able to prevent the adoption of new policies from within the political system, interest groups are not guaranteed success if they try to prevent the government from carrying out its policies. This means that a government that confronts powerful interest groups may have an incentive to act riskily, adopting reforms without offering compensation, in circumstances when they would have offered compensation to a formal veto player.

---

[1] Michael Lipsky (1968, 1145) defined protest as a mode of political action that is "oriented toward objection to one or more policies or conditions, characterized by showmanship or display of an unconventional nature."

Second, political decision-makers sometimes underestimate the strength of powerful interest groups. Such information failures can have important consequences, since governments may decide to ignore the threat that interest groups pose even if it would, in fact, have been more prudent to compromise.

Third, interest groups cannot always be confident in their own *future* strength, since informal power is likely to fluctuate over time. This uncertainty makes it more difficult for governments and interest groups to find viable political compromises, for the interest groups must take into consideration that even if they are currently strong enough to persuade the government to make concessions, the government will have an incentive to revert back to its preferred policy if the power of the interest groups should wane. In these circumstances, agents with informal power might well prefer an immediate confrontation to uncertain promises about future policy. It is likely that Korpi and Shalev had this sort of mechanism in mind when they noted that the transformation that they observed in some European political economies in the postwar period—where strong unions shifted their "conflict strategy" from the economic to the political realm—was only possible where the power of the working class was secure; otherwise, "union movements cannot be expected to seriously countenance the restraint which a 'peaceful' strategy demands" (Korpi and Shalev 1979, 180).

This third mechanism is well known from the more general literature about intertemporal commitment problems that arise from the transience of political power. As Powell (2004) shows, this mechanism is the common denominator in many studies of inefficiencies in political decision-making, from studies of coups and revolutions (Acemoglu and Robinson 2006) to studies of war and civil war (Fearon 2004, 1995).[2]

The first two mechanisms explain why governments will sometimes adopt unilateral reforms even if interest groups will respond by trying to block those reforms. The third mechanism explains, instead, why compensation may not be enough to avoid a political confrontation.

We can think of power sharing as a political solution to these three bargaining problems, which are inherent in the relationship between governments and interest groups. Assuming that power sharing gives the main interest groups in society some measure of formal power, allowing them to influence government policy, power sharing prevents "risky" behavior by political decision-makers and stabilizes expectations about the current and future power of different interest groups. (As I discuss at the end of this chapter, one way to think about the implications of this argument is that according to what we might call a "realist" view of democracy, it is prudent to give

---

[2] Another article that Powell (2004) includes in his survey of this literature is Besley's and Coate's paper on the sources of inefficiency in representative democracies (1998); I discuss that article in Chapter 5.

formal power to groups that would otherwise have strong incentives to try to block reforms.)

The arguments that I have made here lead to three testable propositions.

1. If interest groups are so weak that they cannot hope to ever prevent the government from carrying out its policies, reform capacity is likely to be higher in power-concentration systems than in power-sharing systems. A government in a power-concentration system is free to adopt any policy it wants, but a government in a power-sharing system is sometimes unable to overcome democratic paralysis by compensating losers, for reasons that I discussed in Chapter 3.[3]

2. If interest groups have intermediate strength, however—in the sense that they are strong enough to pose a threat to the government but not strong enough to ensure that the government always offers compensation—reform capacity is likely to be higher in power-sharing systems than in power-concentration systems. In these circumstances, governments may lack incentives to offer compensation (they have incentives to act riskily by adopting unilateral reforms even if this leads to a confrontation with interest groups). Governments may also provoke a confrontation by underestimating the strength of the interest groups, and they may be prevented from making credible promises of compensation due to intertemporal commitment problems. It follows from this argument that we are most likely to observe open displays of informal power—or, in other words, the actual use of alternative political technologies such as protests—in power-concentration systems where interest groups have intermediate strength (which is what the analysis of political strikes shows in the last section of the chapter).

3. Finally, if interest groups have so much informal power that the government always offers compensation—since no one doubts that the interest groups pose a credible threat and will continue to do so in the future—the differences between power-concentration and power-sharing systems are small. In these circumstances, *all* governments have an incentive to offer compensation when they adopt controversial reforms. The intuition behind this claim is simple: when interest groups are very strong, there is essentially no difference between "formal" and "informal" veto players.

---

[3] A related implication is that reform capacity will be higher in power-concentration systems if political conflicts are relatively minor. Since it is typically costly for interest groups to use their informal power, they cannot credibly threaten to do so if a reform only causes minor harm.

It is important to note, before turning to the empirical evidence, that these propositions are based on a rationalist model of political conflict. I treat political protests, and other displays of informal power, as a potential outcome of political conflicts between governments and interest groups over public policy. I also assume that governments and interest organizations behave strategically, balancing two different motivations: on the one hand, they care about policy (governments wish to adopt their preferred policies and interest groups wish to push government policies closer to their own preferred outcomes); on the other hand, they wish to avoid the economic and political costs associated with alternative political technologies. Since I concentrate on trade unions, which are old and highly structured types of organizations, these assumptions are not unreasonable. But they do set the analyses in this chapter apart from many other recent studies of protest politics in the advanced democracies. The literature on political opportunity structures, for instance, has taken a more "cultural" turn, emphasizing the *cultural* openness of political systems rather than formal institutions *per se* (see Hutter 2014 and Braun and Hutter 2016 for a discussion of this literature). I will have little to say about such factors here.[4]

## Labor Market Reforms in Western Europe

The theoretical argument that I developed in the section "Institutions and Interest Groups" suggests that reform capacity should be higher in power-concentration systems if losers from reform have no informal power, but it should be higher in power-sharing systems if losers from reform have enough informal power to threaten to block reform. I begin my assessment of the empirical support for this argument by considering cross-country comparative evidence on reforms. I rely, in this section, on data on labor market reforms in Western Europe that have been compiled by *Fondazione Rodolfo DeBenedetti* (fRDB) in Milan and the *Forschungsinstitut zur Zukunft der Arbeit* (IZA) in Bonn (Fondazione Rodolfo Debenedetti 2010). The fRDB-IZA database provides an "inventory" of important labor market reforms during the period 1980–2007 in fourteen of the fifteen states that were members of the European Union before the enlargement in the 2000s. The database covers two types of reforms—reforms involving employment protection

---

[4] The general idea that "political opportunity structures" influence the politics of protests goes back to social-science classics such as Eisinger (1973), and it has been developed further in more recent studies such as McAdam (1999 [1982]) and Kriesi et al. (1995). My argument that interest groups will refrain from using their informal power to block reforms if they have enough opportunities to influence decision-making *within* formal institutions is related to this literature (see also Nam 2007).

**Table 4.1** Labor market reforms in Western Europe, 1980–2007

|  | Union density | | |
|---|---|---|---|
|  | < 30.3 | 30.3 – 51.5 | > 51.5 |
| Single-party government | 6.5 | 1.7 | 2.4 |
| Coalition government | 6.5 | 4.0 | 6.5 |

The table describes the mean number of structural labor market reforms per country per decade, depending on the type of government and the level of union density (with the observations divided into approximately equally sized groups). The countries included in the analysis are Austria, Belgium, Denmark, Finland, France, Germany, Greece, Ireland, Italy, the Netherlands, Portugal, Spain, Sweden, and the United Kingdom. Both the data on types of government and the data on union density are from Armingeon et al. (2016).

legislation and reforms involving unemployment benefits—and provides information about the characteristics of those reforms.

Table 4.1, which relies on data from the fRDB-IZA database, describes the mean number of "structural" labor market reforms per decade per country (where "structural" means that the reforms affect the entire labor market, not just particular groups) by type of government (single-party or coalition) and by the strength of the trade unions (the cut-off points separate the observations in the fourteen-country sample from 1980 to 2007 into three approximately equally sized groups).

As Table 4.1 shows, the main hypothesis that I derived from the theoretical model—that power sharing is associated with a higher likelihood of reform than a concentration of power if interest groups are powerful—is supported by the evidence: the type of government makes little difference to the adoption of reforms if the trade union movement is weak; but if the trade union movement is moderately strong or strong, coalition government is associated with a significantly *higher* likelihood of reform than single-party government. Reform capacity thus appears to have been higher in countries where power was shared than in countries where power was concentrated.

Table 4.2 relies on the same data set as Table 4.1, but examines a more narrow category of reforms: I now only include reforms that increase the flexibility of labor market regulation (making it easier or cheaper for firms to hire and fire workers) or that render unemployment benefit less generous or more conditional (reducing the amount or duration of benefits, making eligibility conditions stricter, or taking measures that link unemployment benefit receipt to participation in active labor market policy programs). The reason for concentrating on these particular types of reforms is that they are likely to be more controversial, from the point of view of the trade unions, than

**Table 4.2** Labor market reforms: liberalization only

| | Union density | | |
| --- | --- | --- | --- |
| | < 30.3 | 30.3 − 51.5 | > 51.5 |
| Single-party government | 4.8 | 0.5 | 2.4 |
| Coalition government | 5.3 | 3.3 | 4.6 |

The table describes the mean number of structural labor market reforms that increase the rewards from paid work per country per decade. (See also the comments to Table 4.1.)

other sorts of labor market reforms. Again, the observed pattern is very much what one would expect on the basis of the arguments that I have made in this chapter.[5]

These empirical findings rely on descriptive evidence only, and it is possible that the patterns that I have described could be explained by underlying country-level differences rather than the interaction of institutions and interest groups *per se*. Nevertheless, in combination with the case-study evidence on France and the analysis of political strikes that I will report later in this chapter, the findings provide empirical support for the analysis of the relationship among institutions, interest groups, and reforms that I have proposed.

Other cross-country comparative studies of public policies provide additional support for the argument that the effects of formal institutions depend on the strength, or behavior, of interest organizations. Alexiadou (2013) shows, for instance, that in the presence of militant trade unions, coalition governments are more likely to adopt and implement welfare state reforms than single-party governments, since coalition governments are better able to secure broad political agreements (Alexiadou studies the relationship between strike activity, the type of government, and two outcome variables: social security contributions and pension generosity).

## Reforms and Protests in France

I now turn from cross-country comparative evidence to a case study of French politics. The French Fifth Republic is a political system where reforms should

[5] The patterns in Tables 4.1 and 4.2 cannot be explained by the party composition of governments: controlling for left-party cabinet shares makes little difference to the results. But it helps to explain the finding that reforms are more rare under single-party governments than under coalition governments when union density is low (which is inconsistent with the theoretical argument of this chapter). Many of the single-party governments in the top-left-hand cell are left-wing governments.

come easily to governments. With the fall of the Fourth Republic (1946–58) and the inauguration of the Fifth (1958–), France moved from an effectively parliamentary and proportional model of democracy to a semi-presidential, majoritarian model, empowering the executive vis-à-vis the legislature. Philip Williams noted a decade after the transition to the Fifth Republic that "effective government leadership and majority support allowed useful work to be done which was rarely possible amid the shifting combinations of Fourth Republican parties" (Williams and Harrison 1971, 223). A more recent assessment by John Keeler (1993a) reached a similar conclusion (although Keeler also describes some pathologies of the politics of the Fifth Republic that were less apparent to earlier commentators such as Williams and Harrison).[6]

Yet, reforms have *not* always come easily to French governments—at least not in the 1990s and 2000s, which is the period that I will examine here. The main reason is not that reforms were blocked by opposition parties (although France experienced three periods of *cohabitation* in 1986–8, 1993–5, and 1997–2002); the main reason is that trade unions, student organizations, and other interest groups have, from time to time, forced governments to back down from controversial reforms. In the 1990s and 2000s in particular, several important social and labor market policy reform proposals were dropped as a direct result of widespread protests.

This section examines two important reform initiatives in France in the 1990s and 2000s that collapsed due to protests: a failed pension reform (the *Plan Juppé*, which was introduced by Prime Minister Alain Juppé in 1995), and a failed labor market reform (the *contrat première embauche*, or "first employment contract," which was proposed by Prime Minister Dominique Villepin in 2006).[7]

The three mechanisms discussed at the beginning of this chapter are present in both of these cases: the two right-wing governments had incentives to act riskily, adopting unilateral reforms without offering compensation; the two governments underestimated the strength and resolve of the trade unions (and other interest groups, such as student organizations); and when they offered to negotiate with the interest groups, the promises of the two governments were not seen as credible. Following the analysis of these two events, I compare France with two neighboring countries—the United Kingdom and Switzerland—before discussing two *successful* French reform initiatives in order to show how governments may act to build support

---

[6] For Williams's take on the Fourth Republic, see his *Crisis and Compromise* (1964, 257): "The French Parliament was never an efficient legislative machine.... Major reforms could pass only in a major crisis.... By common consent Parliament sat too long and legislated too much."

[7] The section is derived in part from Lindvall (2011), an article published in *West European Politics* on March 10, 2011, which is available online at http://dx.doi.org/10.1080/01402382.2011. 546575.

for reforms in majoritarian systems where interest groups threaten to block reforms.

There is a large sociological literature on the role of protests in France, which is primarily concerned with the inclusion of political protest in the "action repertoire" that defines French political culture (Tilly 1986; Fillieule 1997). This process is clearly an important part of the explanation for the high level of protest activity in France. But the sociological literature has less to say about the variation in protest activity *within* France over time and across policy areas: it does not show why governments sometimes manage to avoid protests, sometimes not. The political science literature, on the other hand, typically describes French politics as a result of the combination of a powerful, autonomous state (Williams and Harrison 1971, 145) and a relatively weak, fragmented trade union movement with low "dialogic capacity" (Culpepper 2002, 782–3; see also Bonoli 1997, 122), rendering negotiations between the government and the trade unions difficult. Again, however, we need to understand why governments sometimes manage to avoid protests, sometimes not.

*Failed reforms*

Consider, first of all, the failure of the so-called *Plan Juppé*, a pension reform that was introduced by the new center-right government in 1995. On November 15 of that year, Prime Minister Alain Juppé presented the National Assembly with a fundamental reform of the social security system, which had been prepared within the Prime Minister's office (Lamothe 2006, 598). At a late stage, a reform of public-sector pensions—including the so-called *régimes spéciaux* for workers in public companies—was added to the government's plan. In Mr. Juppé's speech to the National Assembly, the Prime Minister declared that he wished to harmonize public- and private-sector pensions by raising the minimum number of working years required for a full pension in the public sector from 37.5 to 40, but did not provide further details.

The core elements of the social security reform had been negotiated with the *Confédération française démocratique du travail* (CFDT), France's largest trade union, but the reform of public-sector pensions had not.[8] On the evening of November 15, hours after Mr. Juppé's speech, the main public-sector unions called for a strike directed against the government's unilateral approach to policymaking. The strikes, which began on November 24 and lasted through most of December, turned out to be very damaging

[8] In 1993, Edouard Balladur's government reformed private-sector pensions with the tacit consent of the trade unions (Bonoli 1997, 119; Palier 2005, 234–5; Lamothe 2006, 598). It is interesting to note, as Bonoli (2001) observes, that this reform occurred during a period of *cohabitation*: a period when political power was shared between the left (President François Mitterrand) and the right (Prime Minister Balladur's government).

to the government, economically and politically—not only because several French transport networks were completely shut down, but also because it became increasingly clear that the unions had public opinion on their side (Howard 1998).

The day after the strikes began, the government said that it was open to "dialogue" concerning the pension reform, and the Prime Minister's office announced that it would form a special negotiation commission for this purpose. The commission became operational on November 29, declaring that it sought an "open and in-depth dialogue" with the unions. It soon became clear, however, that the government would have to retreat from the pension reform in order to salvage the general reform of social security, which was the core of the government's reform program. On December 9, the Minister of Labor, Jacques Barrot, met with all the main trade unions (except the left-wing union *Force Ouvrière*, FO) to reassure the unions that the government would, in fact, withdraw its pension reform. On December 10, the negotiation commission was suspended and the pensions reform was dropped. There were further protests for another two weeks, but of the five dominant union confederations in France, only FO and the *Confédération générale du travail* (CGT) continued to support the protests. On December 30, the National Assembly empowered the government to reform social security.

The second reform initiative that I wish to consider is the introduction of the so-called First Employment Contract (*contrat première embauche*, or CPE) in 2006. On January 16, 2006, Prime Minister Dominique de Villepin announced that a new type of employment contract—applying only to workers younger than 26—would be introduced in France. The proposal had several controversial features. Most importantly, it allowed employers to wait up to two years before offering young workers a standard "indefinite" employment contract (*contrat à durée indéterminée*), and during this period employers were free to terminate the contract at will.

When de Villepin made his announcement in January 2006, neither the French trade unions nor France's student organizations had been informed. Once more, the trade unions, even moderate trade unions such as the CFDT, opposed the idea from the start, objecting to the government's "unilateral" approach to policymaking. One week after Mr. de Villepin's announcement, France's main student organizations and trade unions called for national protests against the CPE, beginning on February 7, 2006.

At first, the government did not budge. Mr. de Villepin said that he welcomed a "dialogue" on employment policy in general, but he did not withdraw or alter his proposal. The government's unilateral approach in the early stages of the crisis left the trade unions, as well as France's largest student organization, *Union nationale des étudiants de France* (UNEF), with the impression that the government was not prepared to listen. As the strikes and demonstrations spread, however, and as public opinion turned against the government's proposal, the government said that it was prepared to change certain aspects of the new law. On March 12, the Prime Minister said that he would add "new guarantees": the social insurance rights associated with the CPE would be improved and the new law would be evaluated every six months, in consultation with the social partners. The Prime Minister was also willing to discuss how to "reduce the precariousness of employment" in general. Following a series of meetings with some trade unions and minor student organizations in March, the Prime Minister made further concessions, suggesting that he was willing to discuss the duration of the trial period and the rights of employers to terminate CPE contracts.

But these concessions did not change the position of the main unions and student organizations, who consistently demanded the unconditional withdrawal of the CPE. The final stages of the crisis were managed by an ad hoc committee that was headed by the parliamentary leader of the main right-wing party *Union pour un mouvement populaire* (UMP), Bernard Accoyer. After a number of meetings and conversation among Mr. Accoyer, the ascending right-wing politician Nicolas Sarkozy, and the trade unions and student organizations, President Jacques Chirac withdrew the new law in its entirety on April 10, whereupon the two months of demonstrations and strikes came to an end.

These two events—the failed pension reform in 1995 and the failed labor market reform in 2006—help to illustrate why conflicts between governments and interest groups are more difficult to resolve than conflicts among political parties that operate within the clear boundaries of formal political institutions. In fact, these two events exemplify all of the three mechanisms that I discussed at the beginning of this chapter.

First of all, both Alain Juppé's and Dominique de Villepin's governments acted rashly and riskily: they adopted reforms unilaterally, without offering compensation and without even consulting with interest organizations beforehand. They had political motives for doing so. In Juppé's case, the motive was a desire to introduce significant reforms immediately after the 1995 election, which had resulted in the first unified right-wing government since the socialist François Mitterrand's victory in the presidential election of 1981. In de Villepin's case, the motive was the fierce competition between de Villepin and Nicolas Sarkozy in the run-up to the 2007 presidential election. De Villepin was hoping that a significant legislative victory would give him an edge over Sarkozy (the end result was the opposite: Sarkozy went on to win the presidency).

Second, both governments appear to have underestimated the strength and resolve of the trade unions, expecting that the legislative proposals would not result in significant protests.

Third, although both governments offered to negotiate with the interest groups that opposed the reforms once the protests began, these offers were not seen as credible. By the time that these offers were made, the leaders of the trade unions and the student organizations knew that they were in a strong position since the protests were successful and public opinion was on their side, and they saw the government's invitation to dialogue as an attempt to win time, postponing reform to a more opportune moment, when people had left the streets. In a country like France, where union membership is low, the political strength of the trade unions depends on public opinion and on the ability of the unions to mobilize nonmembers. The unions know, therefore, that their power is fleeting and transient, which exacerbates the intertemporal commitment problems that characterize the relationship between governments and interest organizations.

### Labor law and old-age pensions in neighboring countries

In other European countries, conflicts over pensions and employment law have been resolved differently. The evidence presented so far suggests that important reforms have failed in France since there is a high risk of political confrontations between governments and interest groups in power-concentration systems where interest groups are strong enough to pose a threat to the government's ability to carry out its policies (but not so strong that the government treats interest groups as permanent interlocutors).

To see why the strength of the trade unions matters, consider the reforms that Margaret Thatcher's Conservative government in the United Kingdom introduced in the 1980s. Like France, the United Kingdom is a country with majoritarian institutions (and, therefore, a country with few opportunities for the trade unions to influence policy, at least when the Conservatives are in power). Unlike France, however, the United Kingdom is a country where the unions have become so weak, politically, that they have not posed a political threat to governments.

In the 1970s, the British trade unions *were* strong, both in terms of members and in terms of institutional influence (Grant 2000). Beginning with the appointment of the Conservative Party leader Margaret Thatcher as Prime Minister in 1979, however, the government pursued a deliberate policy of weakening the British trade unions: they were robbed of their earlier institutional access, their rights were curtailed, and, probably as a consequence, they experienced a sharp decline in membership. Especially after the great strike in the mining industry in 1984–5, the union movement was broken politically, and the government was able to push through controversial legislation without effective opposition.

Emmenegger (2014) shows in his comparative study of employment protection legislation in Western Europe that the Conservative government's efforts to change job security legislation—Emmenegger (2014, 204–5) identifies eight separate major legislative initiatives in this area under Thatcher—went hand in hand with efforts to reduce the political influence of the unions. Many job security initiatives were in fact introduced in parallel with anti-union legislation. As a result, the British Conservatives were able to introduce a series of important policy changes without risking further political confrontations.[9]

To see why political institutions matter, consider Switzerland. Like France, Switzerland is a country where trade unions are (potentially) strong enough to organize political protests, but not as strong as the strongest union movements in Europe (which are found in the Nordic countries). Unlike France, however, Switzerland does not have a majoritarian, power-concentrating political system; it has a power-sharing system. As discussed in Chapter 1, the Swiss executive, the Federal Council, is a semipermanent coalition of the four main political parties, and one of those parties, the Social Democrats, is an ally of the trade union movement. Swiss trade unions also get to participate in preparliamentary hearings, giving them an opportunity to express their opinions about legislative proposals in areas such as labor law and pensions before the parliament makes a decision (Mach 2004), and if all else fails, they have the option of calling for a referendum (as they have done in response to some proposed pension reforms; see Häusermann 2010, 186).

As Silja Häusermann (2010) shows in her study of pension reforms in France, Germany, and Switzerland, the Swiss Social Democrats and the largest Swiss trade union confederation, *Schweizerischer Gewerkschaftsbund* (SGB), have by no means always agreed on pension reforms. In particular, the Social Democrats and the unions have often disagreed on what Häusermann calls "recalibration": policy changes that increase the pension rights of groups who are not active in the labor market (179–80). But the unions have typically been closer to the Social Democrats than to other parties, especially when it comes to distributive politics (the "insurance" dimension). The fact that trade unions have so many channels of influence helps to explain why reform initiatives are unlikely to result in protests or other confrontations between governments and unions in Switzerland, unlike in France.[10]

---

[9] As Giuliano Bonoli (2000) shows, the Thatcher government's changes to the pension system were also introduced unilaterally—without consulting either the opposition or interest organizations—in a period when the trade unions had already lost much of their former political clout.

[10] Another example of a country where a pension reform was negotiated among political parties in a way that accommodated the concerns of the most important interest organizations is Sweden. Interestingly, given that Sweden has long corporatist traditions, the Swedish political parties did *not* involve interest organizations directly in the negotiations about the design of the major

## Successful reforms

French governments have not always failed in their efforts to reform old-age pensions and employment law, but successful reforms have often relied on different political methods than the unilateral reform strategies that governments chose in 1995 and 2006.

The *régimes spéciaux*, the special pensions for workers in public companies, were finally reformed in 2007, twelve years after the failed attempt in 1995. After the election of a new President (Nicolas Sarkozy) and the appointment of a new Prime Minister (François Fillon) in the spring of 2007, the French government announced in September that it would propose a reform of the *régimes spéciaux*.

Unlike in 1995, the government sought negotiations with the unions at an early stage. Negotiations between the trade unions and the Minister for Labor, Xavier Bertrand, began in late September 2007. At first, the unions were unhappy with the government's proposals, and they initiated a wave of strikes in October. In early November, however, the conflict was resolved: on November 13, the main left-wing union CGT accepted the government's final proposal, which involved company-based negotiations about compensation for workers whose expectations of a certain pension age and level of pension could no longer be met.

What persuaded the CGT to agree to the government's proposal was a seemingly minor change in the government's position: the government accepted CGT's demand that the government would be represented in the company-based negotiations. The argument that I have developed in this chapter suggests, however, that such promises can be important. One of the key problems when governments negotiate with interest groups is a commitment problem: how to make sure that the interest groups trust the government's promises of compensation. This was why the unions did not see the government's participation in the company-based negotiations as a detail. By 2007, the unions appear to have believed that a reform of the *régimes spéciaux* was unavoidable, perhaps even necessary (the main union confederation, CFDT, accepted the reform from the start). Their main aim, therefore, was to secure compensation for certain categories of workers. The unions needed to be convinced that the government's promises about compensation would be kept before they called off the protests.

The center-right government appointed in 2007 also adopted reforms of labor law. The government introduced a plan to "modernize" the labor

pension reform that was adopted in 1993—in fact, a deliberate decision was made not to do so (Lindvall and Sebring 2005, 1065–6)—but as Anderson and Meyer (2003) have noted, the main trade union confederation, *Landsorganisationen* (LO), was *indirectly* involved since it is closely affiliated with the Social Democrats, who took part in the negotiations.

market in 2008, two years after the confrontation over the First Employment Contract. This reform was again handled very differently from the reforms in 1995 and 2006. Although Sarkozy had declared that he would seek radical reforms of employment protection in the election campaign (Freyssinet 2007, 9), he chose a more cautious approach once he won power: he asked the social partners to initiate negotiations about labor market policy within the framework of a new law on "social dialogue" that the National Assembly had adopted in 2007, as a direct result of the CPE crisis.

The employer organizations and the trade unions reached an agreement on employment protection reforms in January 2008, and this agreement was turned into law in the spring. The policy package extended trial periods and facilitated firing, but also provided for worker training and professional development, introducing, the President said, "flexicurity à la française" (Freyssinet 2007, 3). In other words, the new political procedures appear to have allowed French interest organizations to engage in *quid-pro-quo* reforms—but only as a result of drawn-out and complicated political engineering.

Since political decision-makers often have incentives to act unilaterally, sometimes rashly, France's majoritarian institutions do not adapt easily to compromise. But the two reforms in 2007 and 2008 described here suggest that with thorough preparation, and given that governments manage to reassure interest organizations that promises of compensation will be honored, it is possible, from time to time, to build broader support for reform, avoiding direct confrontations.

### French lessons

Few of the advanced democracies have changed their basic political institutions in the postwar period. The transition from the French Fourth Republic, with its proportional and parliamentary institutions, to the Fifth Republic, a majoritarian and semipresidential regime, is an exception. As a result of the new constitution that was adopted in 1958, the French political system changed fundamentally. In the Fourth Republic, France was ruled by ever-changing coalitions of parties, and most governments only lasted a few months. In the Fifth Republic, strong, ideologically cohesive majority governments have been the norm: with the exception of the three periods of *cohabitation* in 1986–8, 1993–5, and 1997–2002, either the left or (more often) the right has been able to govern alone. France is therefore a particularly interesting test case for a theory of the relationship between political institutions and reform capacity.

Among political scientists, the Fourth Republic, which collapsed as a result of political conflicts over the war in Algeria, has long been seen as a failed political system. Soon after the Fourth Republic's demise, Williams and

Harrison wrote that even before the Algerian war, the Fourth Republic "had been drifting gradually into *immobilisme*" (Williams and Harrison 1961, 165): "Problem after problem was left unresolved because a solution would upset powerful interests, or because the Assembly was too sunk in cabinet crises and outmoded procedures to act." Another expert on French politics, Stanley Hoffmann, noted, similarly, that the Fourth Republic's multiparty system "had no chance of developing stable and coherent governments" since "the problems to be dealt with prevented the formation of lasting majorities." In the end, "French parties, as in the thirties, tended to behave more like pressure groups and to defend the interests of their principal voters" and their "incapacity for defining coherent policy resulted in multiple cabinet crises and undermined the parliamentary system" (Hoffmann 1963, 91).

The Fourth Republic had its achievements, which included France's social insurance system, the *Sécurité sociale* (Palier 2005); the creation of the European Union; and a high pace of economic restructuring and growth. But there is no reason to doubt Williams's and Hoffmann's general assessment of the qualities of the Fourth Republic: as a political regime, it revealed many of the weaknesses and pathologies of power-sharing systems, particularly toward the end, when the Algerian crisis led to the Fourth Republic's demise.

I have argued in this section, however, that the Fifth Republic has its own weaknesses and pathologies. Governments have been stable and strong, allowing the majority party to push legislation through the legislature comfortably and easily. But whereas the parliamentary opposition has been weak, the opposition from civil society has often been powerful and important policy initiatives have frequently been blocked as a result of widespread strikes, demonstrations, and other protests, organized by trade unions and other interest organizations. In a power-sharing system, it is likely that many such confrontations could have been avoided.[11]

## Unions, Institutions, and Political Strikes

I will end this chapter by testing two other implications of the argument that I have made here: the hypothesis that overt displays of informal power should be rare where interest groups are either very weak or very strong and the hypothesis that overt displays of informal power should be rare where

[11] There were politically motivated strikes and other political protests in the Fourth Republic as well, even if the Fourth Republic had a proportional electoral system. But many of these strikes were organized by the *Confédération Générale du Travail*, a trade union confederation with close links to the Communist Party, after the Communist Party was thrown out of the French government in the wake of the political crisis in May 1947 (political strike activity peaked in 1948).

political institutions are more inclusive (that is, where formal power is more evenly distributed).

I test these two claims through an analysis of political strikes in the advanced democracies, drawing on the analyses in Lindvall (2013), but using different data that cover a longer time period. Concentrating on this important category of political protests, I argue that there is a curvilinear, inverted $U$-shaped relationship between union density and the likelihood of political strikes. I argue, furthermore, that the disproportionality of the electoral system has powerful effects on the likelihood of political strikes.[12]

My expectations concerning the relationship among union strength, institutions, and political strikes are informed by the theoretical argument that I made at the beginning of this chapter.

In countries with weak trade union movements, I expect the likelihood of political strikes to be low. Where unions are so weak that they have no chance of defeating the government—that is, forcing the government to abandon or modify the policies or policy initiatives that they object to—they have no incentive to organize political strikes, even if they should disagree strongly with the government's policies or policy proposals. The claim that effective political protests require a basic level of organizational strength is supported by a vast sociological literature on how social movement organizations and interest groups acquire the capacity for mobilization and protest. At first—before the strength of the union movement reaches a point where the other mechanisms that I describe in the following begin to reduce the likelihood of protests—I therefore expect political strike activity to be increasing in union density (as a proxy for the underlying strength of the trade union movement).

In countries with strong trade union movements, I also expect the likelihood of political strikes to be low, but for different reasons. Unlike weak unions, who do not strike since they are not able to, strong unions do not strike since they do not need to. An open confrontation with a strong union movement would be politically costly for any government, particularly if it should lose. Hence, governments in countries with strong union movements have powerful incentives to seek compromises on controversial policy issues in order to avert the latent threat of strikes or other protests. Similarly, unions have strong reasons not to strike if they are able to win concessions from governments through the mere threat of strikes (cf. Murillo 2000, 145, and Murillo 2001, 11). This part of my argument relies on ideas from the comparative literature on class politics and organizational power resources (Hibbs

---

[12] This section is derived in part from Lindvall (2013), an article published in *World Politics* on July 18, 2013, which is available online at https://doi.org/10.1017/S0043887113000142. For another recent study of political strikes in Western Europe, see Kelly et al. (2013).

1978; Korpi and Shalev 1979; Cameron 1984) and the empirical literature on corporatist arrangements in countries with strong union movements (Rothstein 1992). As these studies have all demonstrated, governments in countries with strong unions have historically had powerful incentives to provide the main trade unions with some measure of political power and influence at the decision-making stage rather than having to endure the constant threat of strikes and protests.

In countries with union movements that are neither very weak nor very strong, I expect the likelihood of political strikes to be higher. This hypothesis follows naturally from the arguments that I made already about weak and strong unions: if the likelihood of political strikes at first increases with the strength of the union movement (as unions build the capacity for protest) but later decreases with the strength of the union movement (as governments seek political compromises), it seems likely that there will be some intermediate range of union strength where the second mechanism has not yet begun to counteract the first, and where the likelihood of political strikes is therefore at its maximum. Moreover, as explained in the theoretical section of this chapter, governments are likely to have incomplete information about the mobilization capacity of the trade union movement. They may therefore occasionally underestimate its real strength. Where the trade union movement is either very weak or very strong, such information failures do not increase the probability of political strikes, but in between these extremes, information failures can potentially have important consequences: governments may decide to ignore the objections of the unions even if it would have been more prudent to compromise.[13] Finally, in countries with moderately strong union movements, unions have strong reasons to worry about their own *future* strength. This makes it more difficult for governments and unions to find viable political compromises, for the unions must take into consideration that even if they are currently strong enough to persuade the government to make concessions, the government will have an incentive to revert back to its preferred policy (no concessions) if the power of the unions should decline. In these circumstances, the unions might well prefer an immediate confrontation to uncertain promises about future policy.

Unlike ordinary economic strikes, which are directed against (private or public) employers, political strikes, as defined here, are directed against the policies or policy initiatives of the incumbent national government (cf. Kelly et al. 2013).

---

[13] The idea that strikes are a result of information failures has a long history in economics, going back at least to the work of John Hicks (1963 [1932]).

In Lindvall (2013), I examined the relationship among union density, institutions, and political strikes in the period 1980–2008 on the basis of data that I had compiled for that paper. In this chapter, I have chosen to examine data on general strikes compiled by Banks (2009) and that allow me to examine, instead, the longer period from 1961 to 2008.

Fig. 4.1 illustrates the results of a regression analysis of general strikes that uses union density and the disproportionality of the electoral system as explanatory variables. The disproportionality of the electoral system is included as a measure of power sharing. The idea is that in political systems with few parties, which disproportionality tends to lead to, it is less likely that political parties that represent the same segments of society as trade unions are influential within formal political institutions. (The regression results as such can be found in the Technical Appendix to this chapter.)

Fig. 4.1a—which is based on a model where union density and disproportionality enter separately—describes the estimated likelihood of political strikes in a given country-year as a function of the strength of the trade union movement (on the $x$-axis) and the disproportionality of the electoral system (one curve represents systems with low disproportionality, the other represents systems with high disproportionality).

The curvilinear relationship between union density and political strike activity emerges clearly in this figure. The estimated likelihood of a political strike is low when union density is low or high, but the average predicted probability of a political strike in a given year is high when union density is intermediate. But institutions also matter greatly: the curve for low-disproportionality systems is significantly lower than the curve for high-disproportionality systems, showing that disproportional, majoritarian institutions are associated with a higher likelihood of political strikes. The proportionality of the electoral system—which can be seen as a proxy for the inclusiveness of the political system as a whole—thus has a powerful moderating effect.

Fig. 4.1b is based on a model where the variables measuring the strength of trade unions are *interacted* with the measure of political institutions. As Fig. 4.1b shows, the implications of this more complicated analysis are very similar to the results illustrated in Fig. 4.1a.

The role of formal political institutions in the politics of protest has been documented in other regions. Using data from Latin America, Machado et al. (2011) find a robust negative relationship between the "strength" of political institutions and the propensity for protest. They measure the "capabilities" of the legislature, the "independence" of the judiciary, and the "quality" of the bureaucracy, and create an index of aggregate institutional strength on the basis of these three different measures. In countries where citizens

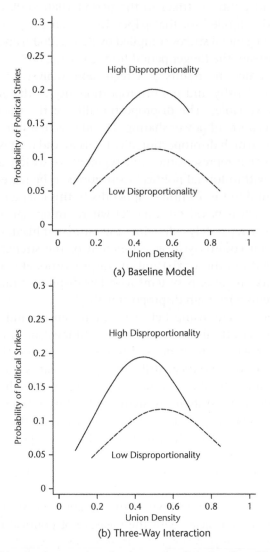

**Fig. 4.1** Political institutions, union density, and political strikes, 1961–2008.

*Comments*: The predicted probabilities are based on two different logistic regression models, which are reported in Table 4.3 in the Technical Appendix to this chapter. Apart from union density and electoral disproportionality, all explanatory variables in the model have been set to their observed values, then average predicted probabilities have been calculated for all observations in the data set (Muller et al. 2014). "Low" and "high" electoral disproportionality correspond to the 10th and 90th percentiles of that variable. Since the range of union density is between 0.17 and 0.85 for countries with low disproportionality and between 0.08 and 0.69 for countries with high disproportionality, I only calculate predicted probabilities for those ranges. The analysis is based on data on general strikes from Banks (2009).

believe that institutions are responsive and effective, they argue, protest is rare; elsewhere, protests are more frequent. Machado et al. also find that citizens who believe that political parties represent their voters effectively are *less* likely to participate in protests where institutions are strong but *more* likely to participate in protests where institutions are weak, suggesting that "just like individuals, parties... choose between the more institutionalized versus the less institutionalized channels" (Machado et al. 2011, 357).

## A Realist's View

In this chapter, I have argued on the basis of theoretical models, cross-country comparative studies, and case studies that where political decision-makers have significant informal power, reform capacity is sometimes higher in power-sharing systems than in power-concentrating systems. Where political decision-makers have negligible informal power, by contrast, reform capacity is likely to be higher in power-concentrating systems, due to the bargaining problems that I discussed at length in Chapter 3.

I began by presenting a simple analysis of structural labor market reforms in fourteen Western European countries, which showed that labor market reforms have been least common when single-party governments have been in power in societies with moderately strong trade unions, just as the theoretical argument suggests. I then presented a case study of French politics, which provided examples of several mechanisms that complicate political bargaining between governments and interest groups: the incentives of governments to act rashly and riskily, the fact that governments do not always have complete information about the strength of the interest groups, and the intertemporal commitment problems that result from the transience of political power. Finally, I used comparative evidence on political strikes to test the idea that political protests are most common in power-concentration systems where interest groups have intermediate strength.

The main implication of the ideas and evidence that I have examined in this chapter is that reform capacity should be highest if the groups in a society that have significant *informal* power also have *formal* power. Since it is easier to reach political compromises within the framework of formal institutions—which serve to stabilize expectations about political strength and power—the most effective way of preventing organized interest groups from using their informal power is to integrate them in the formal political process. Political bargaining between governments and interest groups is almost always complicated by the three problems that I discussed in the context of the case study of France (except in the extreme case of interest groups that are *so* strong that political decision-makers treat them as permanent veto players).[14] If a recurring threat of confrontations between governments and interest groups results in endemic democratic paralysis, reform capacity can be expected to increase if the interest groups—or, more realistically, political parties that represent the same segments of society—are granted some measure of formal power.

There is admittedly something unappealing about this conclusion: it is a realist's view, not an idealist's view. If an interest group uses its informal power to block reforms that a democratically elected legislature has adopted and a democratically appointed executive means to carry out, the interest group interferes, in a sense, with the process of democratic government. We come back, once more, to the difference between justice and political expediency (see Chapter 1). What we can say, on the basis of the analyses in this chapter, is that it is often politically expedient to ensure that informal and formal power are positively correlated in democratic systems.

## Technical Appendix

In this appendix, I extend the game-theoretic analyses that I developed in Chapters 2 and 3 by introducing the possibility that $B$—or, perhaps more realistically, interest organizations representing the same segments of society that $B$ represents—may be able to use "alternative political technologies" to prevent the government from carrying out its policies. The new game-theoretic analyses will show when, if ever, $A$ might have an incentive to offer $B$ compensation even if $B$ has no formal power; when, if ever, $B$ has reason to use alternative political technologies to block reforms; and (combining these two ideas) when, if ever, a power-sharing system has higher reform capacity than a power-concentration system if $B$ has some measure of informal power.

Consider an extension of the power-concentration game (Fig. 2.4) and the power-sharing game with costly compensation (Fig. 3.3). In addition to its formal political power, if any, $B$ now has some measure of *informal* power: $B$ can, if it so desires, use alternative political technologies to try to prevent the government from implementing its policies.[15]

Since it is reasonable to assume that it is less costly—and less risky—for political agents to use their formal power to prevent a reform from being

---

[14] If Charles Lindblom's conclusion (1977, 1982) that business owners and managers always have a privileged position in market-based economic systems with private ownership is correct, these groups do not need formal power: their structural power is enough.

[15] Scartascini and Tommasi (2012), which extends a basic legislative-bargaining model by allowing decision-makers to choose whether to "invest" in either standard political technologies or alternative political technologies, is the theoretical paper that comes closest to the argument that I make here.

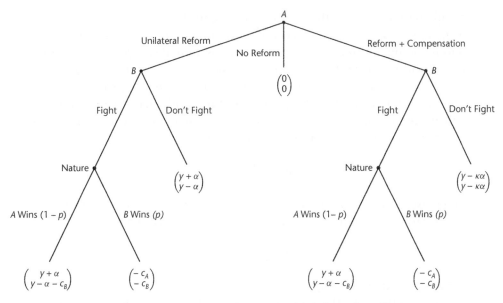

**Fig. 4.2** A power-concentration game with informal conflict.

*adopted* than it is to use informal power to prevent a reform from being *imple-mented*, B never has an incentive to use its informal power in a power-sharing system. The political process in power-sharing systems therefore remains well described by the power-sharing game with costly compensation (see Fig. 3.3 in Chapter 3).

But the political process in a power-concentration system is now best described by Fig. 4.2. In this new power-concentration game, B chooses, if A adopts a reform, whether to accept or fight. Fights are represented by lotteries: with probability $p$, B wins the fight (which means that the reform is not implemented); with probability $1 - p$, A wins the fight (which means that A gets to adopt its ideal policy). *Starting* a fight is costly for B (who pays the cost $c_B$ in the event of a fight). *Losing* a fight is costly for A (who pays the cost $c_A$ if it loses a fight with B).

The power-concentration game with informal conflict has a unique subgame-perfect equilibrium and can be solved with backward induction. If A adopts a unilateral reform, B, comparing the expected payoff of fighting with the expected payoff of accepting the reform that A has adopted, fights if $c_B < p(\alpha - y)$. Otherwise B accepts. If A adopts a reform that includes compensation, on the other hand, $B$ only fights if $c_B < p(\alpha - y) - (1 - \kappa)\alpha$.[16] $A$, taking $B$'s strategies into account, chooses among adopting a unilateral reform, doing nothing, and offering compensation. If $c_B \geq p(\alpha - y)$, $A$ knows that $B$ will never fight, so $A$ adopts a unilateral reform. If $c_B < p(\alpha - y)$, $A$ knows that $B$ will fight in the event of a unilateral reform, so $A$ compares the expected payoffs of fighting, doing nothing, and offering compensation, which are $(1 - p)(y + \alpha) - pc_A$, 0, and $y - \kappa\alpha$. If $y > \kappa\alpha$, so that $A$ prefers compensation to doing nothing, $A$ risks a fight if

$$p < \frac{(1 + \kappa)\alpha}{y + \alpha + c_A}, \tag{4.1}$$

otherwise, $A$ offers compensation. If, on the other hand, $y \leq \kappa\alpha$, so that $A$ would rather do nothing than compensating $B$, $A$ risks a fight if

$$p < \frac{y + \alpha}{y + \alpha + c_A}. \tag{4.2}$$

Otherwise, $A$ does nothing.

The equilibrium in the power-concentration game with informal conflict consequently has the following properties:

(a) If $c_B \geq p(\alpha - y)$, $A$ adopts a unilateral reform and $B$ accepts.

(b) If $c_B < p(\alpha - y)$, $y > \kappa\alpha$, and condition (4.1) is not met, $A$ offers a reform that includes compensation and $B$ accepts.

(c) If $c_B < p(\alpha - y)$, $y \leq \kappa\alpha$, and condition (4.2) is not met, $A$ does nothing.

(d) If $c_B < p(\alpha - y)$, $y > \kappa\alpha$, and condition (4.1) is met, or if $c_B < p(\alpha - y)$, $y \leq \kappa\alpha$, and condition (4.2) is met, $A$ adopts a unilateral reform and $B$ fights.

Fig. 4.3 describes the main implications of the solution to the power-concentration game with informal conflict, as compared with the solution to the power-sharing game with costly compensation.

As Fig. 4.3 shows, there are combinations of parameter values (the white area on the right-hand side) for which reform capacity is higher in power-concentration systems. The reason is that if the costs of compensation are so high that $A$ does not have an incentive to offer $B$ compensation in power-sharing systems, a unilateral reform is the only way forward.

But there are also combinations of parameter values for which reform capacity is higher in power-sharing systems (the dark gray area in the middle of the figure): if $\alpha > y$ and the costs of compensation are lower than the

---

[16] I am assuming that if $B$ is indifferent between fighting and not fighting, $B$ chooses not to fight. Note that if $A$ offers compensation, fighting is off the equilibrium path, for if $A$ has an incentive to offer compensation, $B$ has an incentive to accept.

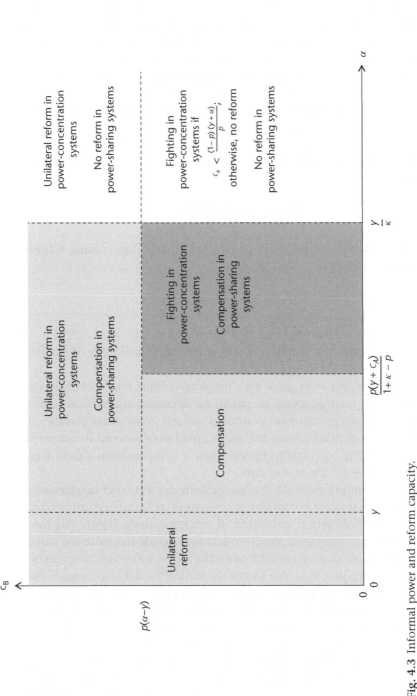

**Fig. 4.3** Informal power and reform capacity.

*Comments*: The dark gray field represents parameter values for which power sharing is associated with higher reform capacity than a concentration of power; the white fields represent parameter values for which power concentration is associated with higher reform capacity than power sharing; the light gray fields represent parameter values for which both types of institutions are associated with high reform capacity (the figure illustrates the results of the analysis of the power-concentration game with informal conflict in Fig. 4.2 and the power-sharing game with costly compensation in Fig. 3.3 graphically). The x-axis represents the level of conflict ($\alpha$). The y-axis represents the costs of fighting for B ($c_B$).

critical value $y/\alpha$, $A$ prefers compensation to doing nothing but $A$ neverthe-less has an incentive to risk a fight rather than compensating $B$. In these circumstances, reforms will *always* be adopted in power-sharing systems (where unilateral reforms are impossible), but they will sometimes fail in power-concentration systems (since there is a risk that $A$ loses a fight).

One of the empirical sections of this chapter examined the relationship between the strength of trade unions and the likelihood of political strikes. The idea that I test in that section—which is that political strikes should be rare when the trade union movement is either very weak or very strong—can also be derived from the power-concentration game with informal conflict in Fig. 4.2. If $A$ prefers compensation to doing nothing, there is equilibrium fighting if

$$\frac{c_B}{\alpha - y} < p < \frac{(1 + \kappa)\alpha}{y + \alpha + c_A}.$$

If, on the other hand, $A$ would rather do nothing than compensating $B$, there is equilibrium fighting if

$$\frac{c_B}{\alpha - y} < p < \frac{y + \alpha}{y + \alpha + c_A}.$$

Either way, there is never fighting if $B$ is very weak (the left-hand side of the two expressions), nor if $B$ is very strong (the right-hand side of the two expressions).

The power-concentration game with informal conflict (Fig. 4.2) illustrates the first of the three theoretical mechanisms discussed in the main text of the chapter: when a government confronts interest groups that threaten to block the government's reforms, the government may have an incentive to act riskily, adopting a unilateral reform even if compensation would have *guaranteed* that the reform would pass.

It would be straightforward to also account for the two other mechanisms. The second mechanism is incomplete information: political decision-makers sometimes underestimate the strength of interest groups, which can have important consequences since governments may decide to ignore the threat that the interest groups pose even if it would be more prudent to compromise. One way to incorporate this idea in the theoretical model is to assume that $A$ does not know the exact value of $c_B$, $B$'s cost of fighting, but instead receives a signal that is sometimes higher or lower than the real value. If the real value is lower than $p(\alpha - y)$ but $A$ believes that it is higher than $p(\alpha - y)$, $A$ will conclude that it is safe to adopt a unilateral reform even if it is not. In a model with incomplete information, the likelihood of fighting is thus higher than it is in the basic model with complete information. But a model with incomplete information would still suggest, as the basic model does, that there will only be fighting in equilibrium if $B$ is neither very weak nor very strong, for if $B$ is either very weak or very strong, $A$ will only draw the wrong conclusion about $B$'s strategy if the signal that $A$ receives about $c_B$ is very far from the real value.

The third mechanism is a commitment problem: it may be impossible for governments to make credible promises to interest groups about future policy, since informal power is likely to fluctuate over time. This idea can be incorporated in the theoretical model by adding a stage to the game, as in the political-turnover game in Fig. 3.7. Imagine that $c_B$ can take two values—a low value, $c_{B_L}$, and a high value, $c_{B_H}$—and that it might change before the compensation that $B$ has been promised has been paid in full (this idea is related to the model of revolutions in Acemoglu and Robinson 2006). If $B$ is offered compensation when $c_B$ is low, $B$ must consider the risk that $c_B$ might increase, and if $B$ does not have an incentive to fight if $c_B = c_{B_H}$,

**Table 4.3** Political strikes, 1960–2008 (regression results)

|  | (1) | (2) |
|---|---|---|
| Union density (0–1) | 8.71*** | 8.65 |
|  | (2.91) | (8.22) |
| Union density$^2$ | −8.54*** | −7.66 |
|  | (3.09) | (8.48) |
| Electoral disproportionality (0–1) | 3.12** | 2.80 |
|  | (1.32) | (5.41) |
| Union density × disproportionality |  | 7.30 |
|  |  | (29.45) |
| Union density$^2$ × disproportionality |  | −15.15 |
|  |  | (35.55) |
| Left party cabinet share (0–1) | −0.21 | −0.21 |
|  | (0.29) | (0.31) |
| Unemployment (0–1) | −0.02 | −0.06 |
|  | (3.66) | (4.53) |
| GDP growth$_{t-1}$ (%) | −0.05 | −0.06 |
|  | (0.05) | (0.05) |
| Corporatism$_{t-1}$ (0, 1) | −0.19 | −0.18 |
|  | (0.52) | (0.53) |
| Union centralization$_{t-1}$ (0–1) | −0.19 | −0.21 |
|  | (0.91) | (0.90) |
| Communist union confederation (0, 1) | 1.69** | 1.68** |
|  | (0.70) | (0.70) |
| Number of previous strikes | 0.01 | 0.01 |
|  | (0.05) | (0.05) |
| Observations | 931 | 931 |
| Countries | 21 | 21 |
| Akaike's information criterion | 585 | 589 |
| Schwarz's Bayesian information criterion | 653 | 666 |

* $p < 0.10$, ** $p < 0.05$, *** $p < 0.01$. Dependent variable: Strike (0, 1). Logit coefficients. Robust standard errors clustered by country in parentheses. All models contain three cubic splines, as recommended in Beck et al. (1998).

*A* will then have an incentive to revert to a policy of no compensation. In these circumstances, *A*'s promises may not be credible, giving *B* an incentive to fight *even if A has offered compensation*. Again, however, the model would suggest that there can only be fighting if *B* is neither very weak nor very strong, for if *B* is very strong, *B* will have an incentive to fight even if the costs of fighting are high, which means that *A*'s promises are credible.

### Regression results

The evidence on the relationship among political institutions, the strength of trade unions, and political strikes that is summarized in Fig. 4.1 is based on the regression results reported in Table 4.3. The model in column 1 in Table 4.3 has the same specification as Model 5 in Table 1 in Lindvall (2013, 554). The model in column 2 in Table 4.3 adds a three-way interaction between union density, union density squared, and electoral disproportionality. As Fig. 4.1 shows, the implications of the two regression analyses are very similar (suggesting, as do the measures of model fit that are reported in the table, that the simpler model should be preferred).

# 5

# Future-Oriented Reforms

In the first three chapters of this book, I argued, contrary to the received wisdom, that power-sharing systems are not necessarily more vulnerable to democratic paralysis than power-concentration systems. Democratic paralysis can be overcome in two ways, by *defeating* or by *compensating* the losers from reform, and although the first strategy is more rarely available to political decision-makers in power-sharing systems, the second strategy is, at least in principle, available to all governments. In Chapter 4, I went further, arguing that if interest groups that operate outside the bounds of formal institutions threaten to block reforms, power-sharing systems may, in some circumstances, have higher reform capacity than power-concentration systems.

This chapter goes further still. Whereas Chapter 4 argued that theories of policymaking need to take into account that political institutions are situated in different societies, this chapter argues that theories of policymaking need to take into account that political institutions, and decision-makers, are situated in time. I show that when it comes to reforms with investment-like properties—policy changes that are associated with short-term costs and long-term benefits (Jacobs 2011, 17–18; Jacobs 2016, 435)—reform capacity can be higher in power-sharing systems than in power-concentration systems. The reason is that investment-like reforms are associated with greater political risks in countries with power-concentration institutions, due to the winner-takes-all character of political competition in those systems. Power sharing can thus be seen as a partial solution to the problem of short-term bias in democracies.

The evidence that I discuss in the chapter's empirical sections suggests that power-sharing institutions do facilitate reforms that are associated with short-term costs and long-term benefits, just as the theoretical argument suggests. I concentrate on two types of future-oriented reforms: reforms of old-age pension systems and reforms of tax systems. Power sharing has historically been associated with high levels of reform capacity in both of these policy areas.

The virtues of power sharing are most apparent, then, whenever the political decisions we take today are associated with short-term costs and long-term benefits (at least if the distribution of those benefits depends on the future distribution of political power). Toward the end of this chapter, I discuss the possibility that there may be a flip side to this argument: the idea that the *vices* of power sharing are most apparent when political decision-makers need to act swiftly and decisively. There is some support for this idea, but many political challenges that appear, at first, to be urgent and short term are, in fact, symptoms of underlying, long-term problems, which suggests that the trade-off between short- and long-term reform capacity is less stark than one might otherwise have expected.

## Democracy's Time Scale

Politicians—and political parties, which are teams of politicians that seek to control the government (Downs 1957, 34)—always worry about the next election, and the next election is rarely more than three or four years away. This is only natural. In fact, one would hesitate to call a system where political decision-makers are completely confident that they will win the next election a "democracy"—the "pro-tempore" character of democracy, Juan Linz notes (1998, 20), is what allows us to distinguish between democracies and other types of political regimes.

But we also want political decision-makers to look to the future, and not just to the next electoral term, but to the one after that. This is why we nod approvingly when we hear of James Freeman Clarke's famous dictum that "[a] politician is a man who thinks of the next election; while the statesman thinks of the next generation" (Clarke 1870, 644). As Linz points out, it is one of the paradoxes of our time that "in an age in which responsiveness to the electorate is sacrosanct, we are more dependent than ever on leaders ... thinking of the future beyond the next election" (1998, 35).[1]

This paradox is not easily resolved. Indeed, an important literature in economics and political science argues that myopia is an inherent and unavoidable flaw in all representative democracies. Besley and Coate (1998) argue, for instance, that since political decision-makers in representative democracies can only control what happens in the current electoral term, not in the next one, they will often refrain from making policy changes that are associated

---

[1] The *Oxford English Dictionary* defines a statesman as "a skilled, experienced, and respected politician." The first definition of "politician" in the same dictionary is "schemer or plotter; a shrewd, sagacious, or crafty person." John Rawls added to Clarke's dictum that political philosophy looks to the "indefinite future" (Rawls 1993, 24).

with short-run costs and long-run benefits: unless they are confident that they, or their supporters, will reap the benefits of future-oriented reforms, they will be reluctant to pay the costs.

There is no perfect solution to this problem: since the possibility of political turnover is a defining characteristic of democracy, the future can never be certain for democratically elected politicians. But it is a problem that is easier to solve in a power-sharing system than in a power-concentration system.

The reason that political decision-makers are reluctant to adopt reforms with short-run costs and long-run benefits is that a future government might adopt policy changes not favorable for the party or parties that are in power now. If that happens, the current government will have paid the short-run costs of a reform, but it will not have reaped the benefits. Consider, for example, the introduction of a new type of tax (an example that I will come back to in the chapter's empirical sections). If a government introduces a new tax, generating new revenues that are available to future governments, but then loses the election, the next government will be able to use the added revenue for its own ends (providing benefits for those who voted for it, for example). The first government will have introduced a new tax, which may not only be politically unpopular but will also be imposed on the government's own supporters; all the benefits, however, go to the second government.[2]

In a power-sharing system, such policy reversals are less likely. As long as power sharing is expected to endure beyond the next election, political decision-makers in power-sharing systems therefore operate in an environment that is much less risky than the winner-takes-all environment of power-concentration systems. Power-sharing institutions thus serve to reassure those who are in power today that they, or the groups that they represent, will be likely to receive a share of the benefits of a reform.

The argument for this view is related to the discussion of commitment problems in Chapter 3. The specific commitment problem examined in Chapter 3 concerned the ability of a reform's winners to make credible

---

[2] There are many other examples of reforms that have short-run costs and long-run benefits. Environmental policy is perhaps the clearest example: the environmental regulations that we introduce today have economic costs in the short term, but the benefits are almost exclusively long term (lower increases in world temperatures, biodiversity, natural resource conservation). Besley and Coate (1998) note that political decision-makers would always have an incentive to invest in the future if it were possible to reach a political compromise between the current policymakers and potential future policymakers (Besley and Coate call this objection "Coasean," citing Coase 1960). They add, however, that the bargaining problems involved in such a compromise would be difficult to solve. "It does not seem unreasonable," they argue, "to presume that transactions costs would hinder the undertaking of such bargains" (Besley and Coate 1998, 152). What I am arguing is that the bargaining problem that Besley and Coate mention is easier to overcome in a power-sharing system than in a power-concentration system (which is the sort of system that Besley and Coate examine in their model).

promises to the losers about future *compensation*. As soon as the compensation comes after the reform itself, I argued, there is an inherent commitment problem in any bargain between winners and losers. The losers will therefore need to be reassured that the winners will not use their political power to block compensation once the reform has been adopted and implemented. This chapter concerns a different sort of commitment problem: the inability of (potential) future governments to reassure the present government that they will not make policy changes that turn the parties currently in power into net losers.

The reason that such commitment problems can often be solved in power-sharing systems is that large changes in the distribution of political power are more rare in power-sharing systems than they are in power-concentration systems. If parties share political power today, it is likely that they will also share power tomorrow. Moreover, opposition parties are often able to influence the legislative process in proportional democracies, even if they are not in government. By helping to resolve the intertemporal commitment problem between present and future governments, a political system based on power sharing consequently enables governments to adopt and implement reforms that would be associated with great political risks in power-concentration systems.

This argument is close in spirit to an argument made by Tommasi et al. (2014), who investigate the relationship between policy "stability" and "adaptability." Tommasi et al. show that in a repeated-games context, the standard idea that there is a trade-off between stability and adaptability does not apply. "Having more veto players," Tommasi et al. observe (223), "means not only more veto players today, but also in the future; this affects the likelihood that any current veto player is also a veto player in the future, and this might lead to different choices than if there was no tomorrow." Tommasi et al. go on to show that having many veto players allows for "efficient adjustments" while preventing "opportunistic adjustments."

My argument is also related to Alan Jacobs's argument about the relationship between political institutions and political "investments" in his *Governing for the Long Term* (2011). Jacobs's argument is based on the idea that institutions have two types of effects (2011, 64). On the one hand, Jacobs argues that the "capacity to invest" (that is, the ability to impose short-term costs for long-term gain) should be higher if politicians are "insulated" (that is, where power is concentrated). Jacobs calls this the "veto-opportunity effect." On the other hand, Jacobs argues that *too much* insulation might render political decision-makers less able to invest in the future, for "where the prospective losers can block policy change, long-term redistribution may be effectively removed from the policy menu." Jacobs calls this the "menu-shaping effect." These ideas are clearly related to the argument that I am developing here.[3]

## Reforming Pension Systems

If the argument that power sharing encourages future-oriented reforms by reducing the risk of future policy reversals is correct, it should be possible to find examples of policy areas where reforms associated with short-term costs and long-term benefits have been adopted sooner in power-sharing systems than in power-concentration systems.

We have already come across policies that fit this description. Consider trade policy (see Chapter 2). In a world where it takes time for economies to adjust, since workers in one sector of the economy cannot immediately find work in another sector of the economy, the full benefits of a trade reform can only be realized in the medium to long term. This is arguably why a power-sharing institution such as proportional representation is associated with a *higher* likelihood of trade liberalization than majoritarian elections. One plausible explanation for this pattern is that proportional representation makes political parties representing potential losers from trade more confident that they will be sufficiently powerful in the future, once the economic structure has changed, to make sure that their supporters get their fair share of the gains of trade.[4]

But in this section, and the next, I would like to concentrate on two policy areas that I have so far only discussed in passing: on the one hand, old-age pensions (one of the main expenditure programs in modern states), and, on

[3] So is Jacobs's general conclusion that "standard veto-point theories of policy change cannot simply be applied 'as is' to understand intertemporal choice in electoral democracies" (2011, 66). My argument is *different*, meanwhile, from the idea that "resoluteness," "the ability of a state to commit to maintaining a given policy" (Cox and McCubbins 2001, 26–31), has economic and political benefits. A large literature in economics and political science argues that although power sharing may be associated with indecisiveness and low reform capacity, it is also associated with resoluteness and stability, which reassures investors (who have less reason to worry about sudden policy shifts that might harm their interests). This general idea is well known from the work of Douglass North and his co-authors on long-term economic development—see, for instance, North and Thomas (1973) and Weingast (1995). This may well be true, but what I am arguing is not that the positive effects of resoluteness (or policy stability, to use Tsebelis's 2002 term) outweigh the negative effects of indecisiveness (low reform capacity). I am arguing, as Tommasi et al. (2014) do, that when policymakers consider policies associated with long-term benefits, power-sharing systems are *more* decisive than power-concentration systems.

[4] On the theory behind this relationship, see especially Katzenstein (1985) and Rogowski (1987); for empirical evidence, see, for example, Persson (2005). Proportional representation is not the only form of power sharing that is correlated with free trade. Lisa L. Martin (2000), for instance, has shown that by constraining the executive, power sharing between the executive and the legislature enhances the credibility of trade deals (trading partners have less reason to worry about policy reversals by executives).

the other, taxation (the main source of revenue in modern states). Both of these policy areas exemplify the challenges that political decision-makers face when they consider future-oriented reforms in democratic systems.

Ever since the 1980s, the reform of old-age pension programs has been one of the most salient political issues in the rich democracies. There has been broad agreement among experts, politicians, and international organizations that established pension programs had become financially and socially unsustainable—primarily, but not exclusively, because of population aging (for useful overviews of reform pressures and reform options in pension politics, see, for example, Schludi 2005, Chapter 1, and Häusermann 2010, Chapter 2).[5]

But all pension reforms involve conflicts between different generations, and between different occupational groups. To maintain the financial stability of the pension system, it is typically necessary for governments to impose short-term costs (by cutting benefits or raising contributions or taxes), and those costs are always distributed among different groups. This combination of future-orientedness (short-term costs and long-term benefits) and distributional conflict makes old-age pensions an important test case for the theoretical argument discussed in this chapter: the argument suggests that if anything, reform capacity in this policy area should be higher in power-sharing systems than in power-concentration systems.

The main conclusion that can be drawn from the literature on pension reform in advanced democracies is indeed that governments in power-sharing systems have been at least as likely to implement significant pension reforms as governments in power-concentration systems, assuming that it has been possible to use compensation mechanisms to build broad support for reforms.

In one of the first major comparative studies of pension reforms in Western Europe, Giuliano Bonoli observed that significant reforms have been possible both in systems with many veto players and in systems with few veto players, noting that even "governments enjoying low levels of power concentration" have been "able to achieve some change" (2000, 172). According to Bonoli, reform *processes* have varied, due to differences between political institutions, but not overall reform intensity. He notes that since "radical and unilateral reforms" are "not 'politically feasible' in countries in which constitutional arrangements encourage power-sharing," governments in such countries "combine retrenchment with quid pro quos" (Bonoli 2000, 173).

A few years later, Martin Schludi (2005, 241) concluded, similarly, that almost all pension reforms in countries with "Bismarckian" pension systems

[5] This section is derived in part from Lindvall (2010b), an article published in *Journal of Theoretical Politics* (DOI: 10.1177/0951629810369524).

have depended either on a deal between the government and the parliamentary opposition or on a deal between the government and the trade unions, and he noted that "even weak governments ... can use their agenda-setting powers to obtain union consent to cuts in pension spending if they offer them attractive compensation payments."

Both these studies concluded that compensation mechanisms allowed governments in power-sharing systems to adopt major reforms. Another five years later, Silja Häusermann's study of France, Germany, and Switzerland (2010) went further, arguing that a high number of formal veto players (such as political parties) and a high number of informal veto players (such as interest organizations) can be a political *asset* for reform-oriented governments: in a multidimensional policy space, Häusermann argued, political fragmentation allows for "coalitional engineering," increasing the likelihood of what she calls "modernizing" reforms (see also Chapter 3 of this book).

Häusermann's study is not alone in reaching the conclusion that having many veto players can be an asset for reform-minded governments. One of the broadest overviews of European pension reforms to date—the *Oxford Handbook of European Pension Politics* (Immergut et al. 2007)—also demonstrates that the veto-player model fails to account for the intensity of pension reform in European welfare states. This is especially noteworthy since one of the editors of the *Oxford Handbook* wrote an early contribution to the literature on veto players and "veto points" (Immergut 1992), and initially expected that a comparative investigation of pension reforms would lend support to such an interpretation: "we were puzzled," Immergut and Anderson note, "that some countries with few veto players and no veto points ... pulled back from controversial pension reforms when they encountered voter resistance [whereas] countries with many veto players and effective veto points ... adopted significant legislation" (Immergut and Anderson 2007, 24).

It was also the case of pensions that led Alan Jacobs to formulate the theory of "governing for the long term" that I discussed earlier: Jacobs's empirical analysis of pension reforms in English-speaking countries led him to conclude, as I noted earlier, that theories of policy change that are based only on the idea of veto points are ill-equipped to understanding intertemporal policy choices (Jacobs 2011, 66).

The evidence from the literature on pension reforms is thus consistent with the argument discussed in the section "Democracy's Time Scale": there is support for the idea that power sharing increases reform capacity when political decision-makers in democracies deal with long-term problems and challenges, since power sharing reduces the risk of future policy reversals and helps to resolve distributional conflicts over reform.

## Reforming Tax Systems

One of the most important developments in comparative politics in recent years is the increasing prominence of the idea that long-run trends in economic and political development depend on *state capacity*, which can be defined as the "degree of control that state agents exercise over persons, activities, and resources within their government's territorial jurisdiction" (McAdam et al. 2001, 78). And one of the most important elements of state capacity is *fiscal* capacity: the ability of states to generate a steady stream of government revenue.

Tax policy is another good example of a policy area where governments make decisions now that are expected to generate benefits in the future. Imposing new taxes is often highly unpopular in the short run, but at least if the imposition of those taxes leads to an increase in fiscal capacity, tax reforms can have significant long-term benefits. At the same time, tax policy is a good example of a policy area where the interests of different groups in society are always in conflict. All states need to raise revenue to perform even their most basic functions—but all tax decisions involve distributional conflicts, for the tax burden always falls on particular individuals and groups.

Political preferences over taxes depend greatly on political preferences over expenditures: what the government *does* with the money it raises. This raises important questions about how governments make decisions about tax policy, and how those decisions should be made. Interestingly, there is an old literature in public finance that deals with this problem. More than a century ago, the Swedish economist Knut Wicksell (1987 [1896]) argued that if the aggregate benefits of government expenditures outweigh the aggregate costs of paying for them, there must logically be a way of sharing those costs that would meet with unanimous approval. Wicksell also makes the interesting point that since political promises are typically not enforceable—and therefore not, in a real sense, binding—it is desirable to make decisions about revenue and expenditures simultaneously, as a package. Furthermore, Wicksell argues that proportional representation—which had not been introduced by a single national government when he wrote his book—has important merits since it is consistent with the principle that packages of expenditure and tax decisions should be able to attract broad-based support.[6]

There is a strong resemblance between my general argument that power sharing leads to higher reform capacity when the distributional effects of

---

[6] I am grateful to Per Andersson for bringing Wicksell's book to my attention.

reforms depend on the actions of future governments, since it reduces the risk of future policy reversals, and Wicksell's normative argument that proportional representation is an appropriate decision mechanism in the area of tax policy.

There is also a strong resemblance between my argument about power sharing and the argument behind one of the few formal models of fiscal-capacity building in contemporary economics and political science: the model of state capacity that has been developed by Besley and Persson (2010, 2011). One of the key mechanisms in Besley and Persson's model is that even if high levels of fiscal capacity provide net benefits for society, political decision-makers will be reluctant to increase state capacity, including fiscal capacity, if they worry that future policymakers will use that capacity for political purposes that the current government disapproves of (by using the resources of the government to benefit their own supporters exclusively, for instance).

For this reason, Besley and Persson suggest that "cohesive" political institutions lead to larger investments in fiscal capacity. They expect "democracies to be more cohesive than autocracies; parliamentary forms of government to be more cohesive than presidential forms of government; and proportional electoral systems to be more cohesive than majoritarian electoral systems," whereas "federal governments may or may not be more cohesive than unitary governments" (Besley and Persson 2011, 32). The mechanism that Besley and Persson have in mind is similar to the mechanism that I discuss here: reforms become more likely if political decision-makers have fewer reasons to worry that future decision-makers might use the benefits of the reforms to further their own, particular interests.

Let us now consider some evidence on these sorts of conflicts, to see if more cohesive governments have indeed been better able to introduce tax reforms that resulted in long-term increases in fiscal capacity.

I begin with the first major tax innovation of the late-modern period: the personal income tax. One might think that Besley and Persson's argument is undercut by the fact that income taxes were often introduced by authoritarian governments, not democratic ones, as both Aidt and Jensen (2009) and Mares and Queralt (2015) have demonstrated.

In a recent paper, however, Thomas Brambor (2016) examines how political institutions and political conflicts at the time of the adoption of the income tax influenced future levels of fiscal capacity. Brambor shows that although governments in democracies were not more likely than governments in autocracies to *introduce* income taxes, the tax *revenues* generated by income taxes turned out to be significantly higher over time in countries where income taxes were introduced in democracies. These legacies of early income-tax reforms remained in place many decades after these reforms were first adopted.

This suggests that in political systems where political power was historically shared more widely, tax reforms led to higher effective fiscal capacity in the long term than they did in countries where power was historically more concentrated. Systems where power is concentrated may be able to act quickly, but they seem to be less able to solve long-term political and economic problems.

I turn next to another major shift in taxation: the shift from income taxes to consumption taxes. Per Andersson (2016) has recently developed an argument about how political institutions and party politics have combined to shape the structure of twentieth-century tax systems. Although consumption taxes have many advantages, since they are easy to collect and have fewer distortionary effects than many other types of taxes, Andersson notes that they have one important drawback: they are typically more regressive than direct taxes, which means that if redistribution is an important political objective, governments will be reluctant to introduce them.

Andersson (2016) argues, however, that the level of power sharing, specifically the electoral system, is important to take into account when analyzing the choices that governments have made about income taxes. His argument is concerned specifically with the behavior of parties on the left. As authors such as Steinmo (1993) and Beramendi and Rueda (2007) have shown, left-wing parties have been more likely than right-wing parties to rely on consumption taxes. Andersson shows however, that in majoritarian political systems, the left has in fact *resisted* the introduction of consumption taxes; in proportional systems, in which the influence of the opposition is greater, the left taxes consumption more than income.

The explanation is in all likelihood that the left is happy to introduce, and raise, consumption taxes as long as it is confident that the revenue will in fact be used for the purposes that it seeks to achieve. But if the left fears that other parties will use the revenue raised for completely different purposes— a risk that is greater in majoritarian systems—it will choose differently. The evidence suggests, in other words, that political institutions matter greatly for the tax policy choices that governments make.

The value of high fiscal capacity is that it becomes a matter of *choice* whether taxes are raised. Clearly, the value of a tax reform—both from the point of view of parties and from the point of view of social welfare—depends on what the money raised is used for. But it is prima facie a good thing if governments are able to raise revenue effectively to meet changing economic, social, and political needs. One of the main obstacles to reforms that increase fiscal capacity is that governments fear that their opponents will use the new revenue to further their own particular agendas. Power sharing guards against this risk.

## Crises

In the two sections "Reforming Pension Systems" and "Reforming Tax Systems," I argued that the virtues of power sharing are most apparent when political decision-makers consider reforms that have short-term costs and long-term benefits, since such reforms are associated with great political risks in power-concentration systems (at least if the distribution of the long-term benefits depends on the actions of future policymakers). I now consider the corollary argument that the *vices* of power sharing are most apparent when political decision-makers face urgent problems and need to act quickly and decisively.

One observation that lends force to this argument is that power-sharing democracies have historically proven to be unstable during national security crises (when governments must make swift decisions about diplomatic initiatives and the deployment of military forces) and during financial and economic crises (when governments must respond to rapidly unfolding economic events). The collapse of the Fourth Republic in France—which I discussed in Chapter 4—is an example of a power-sharing democratic regime that fell as a result of a crisis involving national security (the war in Algeria that began in 1954). The collapse of the Weimar Republic in Germany is an example of a power-sharing democratic regime that fell as a result of an economic crisis (the Great Depression of the 1930s).[7]

One way to explain these patterns is by referring back to the discussion of bargaining problems in power-sharing systems in Chapter 3. Political decision-makers need to solve two difficult problems when they seek to resolve conflicts over reform by compensating losers: they need to make sure that the costs of compensation are low and they need to make sure that the winners are able to commit to compensating the losers. Solving these problems takes time, and when urgent action is needed, the time that policymakers have to reach viable compromises may not be enough. In power-concentration systems, it is often possible for political decision–makers to

---

[7] Bernhard et al. (2001) show that majoritarian democracies have generally been more resistant to economic stress than proportional democracies, whereas proportional democracies, by contrast, have been more resilient when the economy was growing. When it comes to wars and other national security crises, it is worth noting that going back at least to the Roman republic—which appointed especially powerful magistrates, *dictators*, in times of war—many states have from time to time introduced wartime legislation that temporarily concentrated powers in the executive. (On legislation empowering executives in parliamentary systems during and after the First World War, see especially Tingsten 1926, 1930.)

ignore the losers, which is a quicker, more direct political strategy; figuring out how to compensate the losers is a more complicated and demanding strategy.[8]

It is possible that parties and voters are prepared to accept drastic policy changes when a looming crisis is seen as a great threat, mitigating the problems that I have just described. Weyland (1998) examines popular support for neoliberal economic reforms in Latin America and finds that voters accept draconian adjustment programs if they believe that those programs will help to overcome a deep economic crisis. In the short run, Weyland finds little support for the "compensation hypothesis," according to which governments build support for reforms by using social policy to compensate losers. He finds, however, that in the medium to long run, social benefits were used to *consolidate* support for neoliberal economic policies. The idea that the need to act decisively in the first phase of a deep economic crisis must be balanced against the need to adopt a balanced policy response in the medium run recurs in Andrew MacIntyre's study of the East-Asian financial crisis (2001), which finds that systems with a small number of veto players fared worse than systems with an *intermediate* number of veto players.

On balance, however, it seems likely that the weaknesses of power sharing do become more apparent during crises, when political decision-makers need to act swiftly to avoid some great harm. Evidence from the Great Depression supports this idea. Very few countries adopted expansionary fiscal policies in response to the Great Depression. One of the few countries that did was Sweden, but even in Sweden, it took until 1933—several years into the crisis—before it was possible for the government to build enough support in parliament for such a policy. As I have discussed elsewhere (Lindvall 2012), the main reason for this political disagreement was that politicians were concerned about the indirect political and distributional effects of new economic policies, *not* their direct economic effects. It was widely expected that new programs for economic stimulus would have far-reaching political effects, which complicated interparty bargaining.[9]

---

[8] Andersson and Lindvall (2016) propose a different mechanism that might also help to explain why it is difficult for political decision-makers to respond to urgent problems in power-sharing democracies. To the extent that crisis management means adjusting taxes and spending to the needs of the moment, political decision-makers in power-sharing systems may worry that other parties will use a crisis as an opportunity to "lock in" their favorite policies (as Rahm Emanuel, Barack Obama's incoming chief of staff, said two weeks after the presidential election in November 2008, "You never want a serious crisis to go to waste"; see *Wall Street Journal* 2008). The basic mechanism is again a commitment problem: since the party that benefits the most from a short-term shift in policy cannot commit to returning to the status quo once the crisis is over, it may be rational for the group that is harmed the most by the short-term shift in policy to block effective crisis-management measures.

[9] In the Great Recession of the 2000s, by contrast, political parties were less concerned about the indirect political effects of expansionary fiscal policies, which helps to explain why governments were so willing to launch stimulus programs in the recent crisis.

## A Time to Judge Every Deed

This chapter has argued that power-sharing institutions provide a partial solution to an important political problem in democratic policymaking: the problem of myopia, or shortsightedness. When reforms have long-term benefits for society but are associated with significant short-term costs, governments are more likely to adopt a reform in a power-sharing system than in a power-concentration system, assuming that the bargaining problems discussed in Chapter 3 can be solved effectively. In the Technical Appendix, I extend the game-theoretic models introduced in Chapters 2 and 3 to show how the intertemporal distribution of the costs and benefits of a reform combine with the costs of compensation to shape political conflicts, illustrating the chapter's main points.

Whereas the virtues of power-sharing systems are most apparent when political decision-makers consider reforms that have short-term costs and long-term benefits, the vices of power sharing are most apparent during crises, when time is of the essence and political decision-makers need to act swiftly and decisively to avoid some great harm.

From a normative point of view, then, the question that we need to ask ourselves is this: Are we living in a world where short-term problems dominate—where governments must often respond to urgent crises that require rapid shifts in public policies to respond to immediate needs—or are we living in a world where long-term challenges dominate, requiring governments to set aside resources now to improve future welfare?

The archetypical example of the first kind of world is a world of recurring wars and economic crises. The archetypical example of the second kind of world is a world of environmental problems, demographic change, and technological development. In the first kind of world, power-concentration institutions seem to be preferable: the evidence that power-sharing institutions are at least slightly inferior when responding to sudden crises seems both strong and compelling. In the second kind of world, however, power sharing seems preferable: the main threat to all political efforts to find appropriate solutions to long-term problems is the fear of opportunistic behavior by future governments.

One thing that we should consider, when pondering this problem, is that very few challenges are exclusively short-term. Some economic crises are truly urgent—as are some national security crises—but many other problems that may appear to be short-term in nature are in fact symptoms of underlying long-term problems.

Consider natural disasters. Natural disasters may appear to be archetypical short-term problems: when the storm blows, the tide rises, and the flood comes, it is important to act quickly. As the literature on the political economy of natural disasters shows, however, responding to natural disasters is a long-term challenge, for investments in infrastructure and disaster preparedness matter greatly to how much harm natural disasters cause (Cohen and Werker 2008).

If the ability of governments to respond effectively to natural disasters depends, at least in part, on prior investments, the actual damage of a natural disaster will depend on a combination of two factors: on the one hand, long-term policies (which power-sharing systems are well-equipped to manage) and, on the other hand, short-term responses (which power-concentration systems are more likely to handle well). This may be why the relationship between political institutions and the outcomes of natural disasters is weak: Busch (2012) finds no relationship between the electoral system and disaster deaths, and suggests that this finding is best explained by the fact that the electoral-system effects of "representation" and "accountability" cancel each other out.[10]

The ideas and evidence discussed in this chapter confirm the widely held belief that the relative strengths of power-concentration systems are most apparent when political decision-makers must act quickly and effectively. As Schmidt (2002, 150) put it in a review article about the performance of democracies, "Challenges requiring swift response, the rapid development of political alternatives and rapid decision making tend to overburden the non-majoritarian democracies." But I have also shown that power-concentration systems have their own weaknesses: conflicts over policy changes associated with long-term benefits and short-term costs are difficult to resolve in those systems due to the winner-takes-all character of political competition. There may be a trade-off, in other words, between short-term and long-term reform capacity.

## Technical Appendix

In this appendix, which extends the simple game-theoretic models introduced in Chapters 2 and 3, I show how political decision-makers act when the gains of a reform are only realized in the long term, and future governments can influence the distribution of those gains. Fig. 5.1 describes the power-concentration game with investments, which is a simple game-theoretic representation of this problem.

As before, the game begins with party $A$ choosing a policy (doing nothing, adopting a unilateral reform, or adopting a reform that includes compensation for the losers).

---

[10] It is likely that a similar argument could be made about antiterrorism policy.

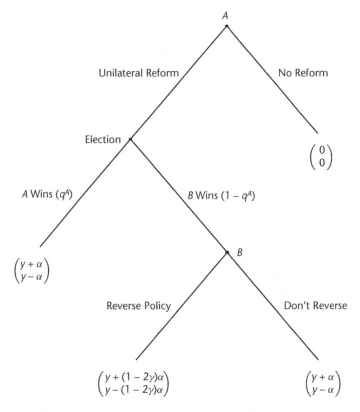

**Fig. 5.1** A power-concentration game with investments.

When the policy choice has been made, elections are held (as in the political-turnover game examined in Chapter 3; see Fig. 3.7). $A$ wins the election with probability $q^A$ and $B$ wins the election with probability $1 - q^A$.

As in the political-turnover game, the effects of the policy decision made at the beginning of the game is either realized before the election or after the election, or both. The proportion of the policy's effects realized *after* the election is denoted $\gamma \in [0, 1]$.

If the effects are not fully realized before the election, the new government appointed after the election is able to change the policy. Such a decision affects the proportion of the policy's effects realized in the postelection period. In the model examined here, however, the government is able to change policies in a more radical fashion than in the political-turnover game. In the political-turnover game, the only policy change that the government appointed after the election could introduce was to reverse the decision to compensate the losers (if such a decision was made). In the power-concentration game with investments, by contrast, the government appointed after the election is able to change the reform's distributional profile completely, so if $B$ wins power, and none of the effects of the reform are realized before the election, $B$ can change the policy so that $A$ gets the payoff $y - \alpha$ and $B$ gets the payoff $y + \alpha$. This setup is meant to illustrate the fact that $A$ might take a risk when adopting a reform: if $B$ wins power, $B$ is able to use the benefits generated by the reform for its own purposes.

Since $A$ never has a reason to compensate $B$ in the power-concentration game, I concentrate on the choice between doing nothing and adopting a unilateral reform. If $A$ adopts a reform, the proportion $1 - \gamma$ of the full effects of the reform are realized before the election, giving $A$ the combined payoff $(1 - \gamma)(y + \alpha)$ for that period. Then elections are held. If $B$ wins the election, $B$ has the opportunity to change the distributional profile of the reform (if one was adopted), changing the proportion of the effects of the reform realized after the election. If $B$ changes the distributional profile of the reform, $A$'s and $B$'s payoffs after the election are $\gamma(y - \alpha)$ and $\gamma(y + \alpha)$. The payoffs described in Fig. 5.1 are the total payoffs for $A$ and $B$ for each "path" in the game tree.

The game can be solved with backward induction. If $B$ is in power after the election, $B$ always reverses the policy (making the policy as beneficial as possible for $B$). $A$ therefore needs to take the likelihood that $B$ might win the election into account when choosing a policy at the beginning of the game. The expected benefit of a unilateral reform for $A$ is $y + (1 - (1 - q^A)2\gamma)\alpha$, which means that $A$ adopts a reform if

$$\alpha < \frac{y}{(1 - q^A)2\gamma - 1} \tag{5.1}$$

In other words,

(a) if condition (5.1.1) is met, $A$ adopts a reform, and if $B$ wins the election, $B$ changes the distributional profile of the reform;

(b) if condition (5.1.1) is not met, $A$ does nothing.

If we assume, to keep things as simple as possible, that $A$ and $B$ share power both before and after the election, which means that no party in a power-sharing system is ever able to adopt policy changes unilaterally, the government that chooses whether to adopt a reform does not have to worry about future policy reversals, so the political process is still well represented by the power-sharing game with costly compensation (see Fig. 3.3). Even if this assumption about the enduring nature of power sharing is relaxed, however—as in the political-turnover game in Chapter 3—power-sharing systems have higher levels of reform capacity than power-concentration systems in some circumstances as long as the probability that one of the parties wins power single-handedly is *lower* in power-sharing systems than in power-concentration systems, which seems like a reasonable assumption to make.

In the power-sharing game with costly compensation, reform capacity, or $R$, was equal to $\frac{1}{2\kappa}$. In the power-concentration game with investments, by contrast,

$$R = \frac{1}{4(1 - q^A)\gamma - 2}.$$

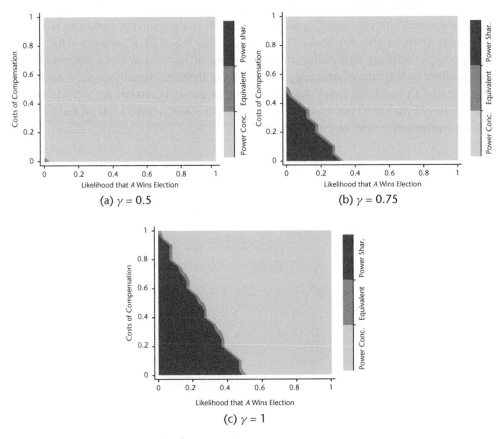

**Fig. 5.2** Investments and reform capacity.

*Comments*: Darker fields represents combinations of parameter values for which power sharing is associated with higher reform capacity than a concentration of power (the figure illustrates the results of the analysis of the power-concentration game with investments and the power-sharing game with investments graphically). The x-axis represents the likelihood that $A$ will win the next election. The y-axis represents the costs of compensation ($\kappa$).

What these analytical results tell us is that a failure to reform occurs for *different reasons* in the power-concentration game with investments (Fig. 5.1) and the power-sharing game with costly compensation (Fig. 3.3). In a power-concentration system, reform capacity is low if $\gamma$ is high (most of the beneficial effects of a reform are realized in the future) and $q^A$ is low ($A$ is unlikely to win the next election). In these circumstances—when a reform has investment-like properties and when $A$'s political position is not secure—$A$ worries that it will turn out to be a loser from reform, in the event that $B$ wins power. In a power-sharing system, by contrast, reform capacity is low, as before, when the costs of compensation ($\kappa$) are high. The *relative* reform capacity of power-concentration and power-sharing institutions thus depends on three factors: $\gamma$, $q^A$, and $\kappa$.

This is exactly what Fig. 5.2 shows. The dark gray areas in Fig. 5.2 represent parameter values for which reform capacity, $R$, is higher in the power-sharing game than in the power-concentration game. Fig. 5.2c represents what is perhaps the most interesting situation: when *all* of the gains of a reform are realized in the future (after the next election). In these circumstances, assuming that the costs of compensation are low, power-concentration institutions are only superior to power-sharing institutions when $A$ has a high probability of winning the next election ($q^A > 0.5$).

# 6

# Reform Capacity

Reform capacity, the ability of political decision-makers to adopt and implement policy changes that benefit society as a whole, is an important problem in politics. It is an *important* problem since yesterday's policies are not always equipped to address today's concerns. It is a *problem* since almost all efforts to adjust public policies to new economic, social, and political circumstances are politically contested: there are winners and there are losers, and the losers have strong reasons to oppose reforms—including reforms that would make most people better off.

According to one view of democratic politics, which I have called the concentration-of-power hypothesis, the only feasible solution to the problem of reform capacity is to build institutions that enable governments to *ignore* losers from reform. In this book, I have examined a very different idea about the relationship between political institutions and reform capacity. According to this alternative view, which we can call the power-sharing hypothesis, there is another solution to the problem of reform capacity: to build institutions that enable governments to *compensate* losers.

In this chapter, I discuss the main conclusions of my investigation into the relationship between political institutions and reform capacity. I then consider the broader implications of the book's argument for general theories of democratic institutions. Finally, I examine some of the economic, social, and political problems that the advanced democracies are facing today. I discuss the conflicts between winners and losers in the modern economy, which show, in my view, how crucial it is for democracies to come up with ways of compensating losers. I also discuss some current trends in democratic governance that have troubling implications for the ability of governments to overcome conflicts over reform.

## Main Lessons

This book started with the observation that if political decision-makers are able to compensate losers—the groups that expect to be harmed by reforms—it should in principle always be possible to overcome democratic paralysis in power-sharing systems, even if political parties are engaged in divisive conflicts. As long as the losers can be compensated, therefore, power sharing does not necessarily lead to low reform capacity. Even if we care greatly about the "firmness and efficiency of government," as Alexander Hamilton did, we need not conclude that power should be concentrated, between elections, in a single governing party (see Chapters 1 and 2).

But governments in power-sharing systems sometimes fail to adopt reforms. There are power-sharing systems where all kinds of minor disagreements among political parties lead to democratic paralysis—which is the defining characteristic of low reform capacity—and historically, some power-sharing systems have been so vulnerable to paralysis that powerful groups in society lost faith in the basic principles of democratic government.

Chapter 3, which asked why governments sometimes fail to adopt desirable policy changes, identified two types of problems that political decision-makers need to solve when they build support for reforms. The first problem is that political compromises may be associated with significant economic and political costs, and reform capacity inevitably declines, in power-sharing systems, when those costs increase. The second problem is that it may be difficult for the winners to commit to compensation, which means that their promises of compensation are not always credible.

Compensation, as a political strategy, therefore places high demands on political institutions. Chapter 3 ended on a slightly pessimistic note: yes, it is in principle possible to overcome democratic paralysis by compensating losers, but if winners and losers have sharply diverging interests and preferences, it is difficult in practice. High reform capacity, in power-sharing systems, requires a combination of institutions that facilitates political bargaining between winners and losers. Some of those institutions can be altered in the short term, which means that political agents are able to improve reform capacity on their own accord. But others, such as basic constitutional provisions, are more resistant to change. Moreover, given realistic assumptions about how far bargaining costs can be reduced and how well intertemporal commitment problems can be solved, there is always *some* level of political polarization beyond which political bargaining is brought to a halt.

The message of the following two chapters, Chapters 4 and 5, was more upbeat. In these chapters, I argued that if political decision-makers in power-sharing systems manage to solve the two bargaining problems discussed in

Chapter 3 satisfactorily (keeping the costs of compensation low and committing to future policies), power-sharing systems have certain advantages over power-concentration systems. The main vice of power-sharing systems—the fact that governments are often compelled to compensate losers—can, in some circumstances, become a virtue, since the "inclusive" strategies that governments rely on in power-sharing systems sometimes allow governments to accomplish things that they could not otherwise accomplish. In Chapter 4, I argued that power-sharing systems may have higher levels of reform capacity than power-concentration systems when strong interest groups, operating outside the bounds of formal institutions, threaten to block controversial reforms. In Chapter 5, I argued that power-sharing systems may have higher reform capacity than power-concentration systems if reforms have short-term costs and long-term benefits, since governments have fewer reasons to worry about the possibility of future policy reversals in systems where power is shared among several parties.

Although Chapters 4 and 5 are concerned with different sorts of problems, there is a basic similarity between the arguments that I make in those two chapters. In both Chapter 4 and Chapter 5, the main claim that I am advancing is that if we move beyond a "snapshot" view of political decision-making, by situating political institutions in space (Chapter 4) and in time (Chapter 5), we find that power-sharing institutions allow political decision-makers to develop broader political compromises than power-concentration institutions: compromises that are more socially acceptable (that do not provoke an adverse response from social actors) and more sustainable (that reduce the risk of policy reversals by future governments).

So, what have we learned? Does effective government require a concentration of power?

The answer to that question depends on how worried we are about the vices of power-sharing systems (Chapter 3) and how much we care about their virtues (Chapters 4 and 5). In countries that have built—or are able to build—institutions that allow political decision-makers to keep the costs of compensation low, and to make credible promises about future policies, the virtues are likely to outweigh the vices. In such societies, power sharing is associated with higher reform capacity than a concentration of power. In countries that cannot easily put those sorts of institutions in place, however, the vices may well outweigh the virtues. In such societies, a concentration of power leads to higher reform capacity.

The answer also depends on the nature of the economic, social, and political challenges that governments confront. When most economic and social problems are long term, and when interest groups can credibly threaten to block reforms, power-sharing institutions are more likely to lead to higher reform capacity than power-concentration institutions. But if political decision-makers must deal with recurring crises that call for swift and decisive action, while interest groups are fragmented and weak, power-concentration institutions tend to perform better.

A more general lesson of the ideas and evidence that I have discussed in this book is that we learn a great deal about politics by studying compensation. As discussed in Chapter 1, my approach to the problem of reform is inspired by a classic literature in welfare economics, which treats compensation as a central concept and problem. In "The Foundations of Welfare Economics," one of the papers that introduced the idea that later became known as the Kaldor–Hicks principle, John Hicks wrote that the "practical advantage" of the approach that he proposed was "that it fixes attention upon the question of compensation" (1939, 711). He noted that throughout history, when governments have adopted and carried out reforms, "the advance has usually been made amid the clash of opposing interests, so that compensation has not been given, and economic progress has accumulated a roll of victims, sufficient to give all sound policy a bad name." He suggested, therefore, that economists should accustom themselves to "thinking of every economic reform in close conjunction with some measure of compensation."

The motivating idea of this book is that by thinking of reforms "in close conjunction with some measure of compensation," we also understand politics better.

## From Reform Capacity to Good Government

As I discussed in Chapter 1, the question that this book has sought to answer is a narrow one. I have not developed a theory of policy change in general, as Tsebelis (2002) did; I have instead developed a theoretical argument about the ability of political decision-makers to adopt and implement reforms (policy changes that benefit society as a whole). I have not studied the general performance of democratic systems (the macro-level relationship between political institutions and economic and social outcomes), as Lijphart (1999, 2012), Bueno de Mesquita et al. (2003), Roller (2005), and Gerring and Thacker (2010) did; I have instead sought to provide a precise theoretical and empirical account of how democracies deal with particular types of conflicts.

But the ideas and evidence that I have introduced in this book have important implications for broader discussions about the advantages and disadvantages of different types of democratic institutions.

I already discussed one of those implications in Chapter 1. For decades— centuries, even—scholars of politics have disagreed on how power and authority should be allocated among institutions and political parties in well-ordered democratic systems. In this long-standing debate, political scientists often set two ideal-typical models of democratic government against one another: "majoritarian" democracies on the one hand and "proportional," or "consensual," democracies on the other. The choice between these two ideal-typical models is normally described as a trade-off: by choosing one of them, you win some things, but you lose other things. Reform capacity is typically treated as a virtue of majoritarian, power-concentrating systems. Proportional systems have other virtues (especially representativeness and responsiveness), but it is often assumed that if we want those things, we must sacrifice reform capacity.

This book casts doubt on that assumption. Both power-concentration and power-sharing systems are vulnerable to democratic paralysis, but for different reasons. Power-sharing systems are vulnerable to democratic paralysis when political decision-makers are unable to keep the economic and political costs of compensating the losers low, or when the "winners" are unable to commit to future policy choices. These two problems become more acute, as I discussed in Chapter 5, when reform is urgent. Power-concentration systems, by contrast, are vulnerable to democratic paralysis when strong interest groups threaten to block reforms, or when governments have the opportunity to "invest" in the future by adopting reforms that have short-term costs but long-term benefits.

In other words, power-concentration and power-sharing systems each have their own pathologies.

These ideas and findings do not settle the debate between the proponents of power-concentration institutions and those of power-sharing institutions, of course. In my view, however, they change the *terms* of that debate. Before we assess the advantages and disadvantages of different types of political systems, the question we should ask is whether political decision-makers are able to solve the bargaining problems that might prevent compromises between winners and losers (Chapter 3). We will not understand the relationship between institutions and reform capacity unless we first examine that question.

This brings me to a second implication of the ideas and evidence that I have examined in this book. One of the most recent attempts to assess the general performance of democracies is Gerring's and Thacker's study *Centripetal Democratic Governance* (2010), which argues that the optimal political system combines a unitary state structure (as opposed to federalism), a parliamentary system (as opposed to a presidential one), and a proportional, closed-list electoral system (as opposed to a majoritarian one). Gerring's and Thacker's general idea is that the optimal political system is defined by both *inclusion* and *authority*: a multitude of groups, with different interests and values, are integrated in the political process, but the political system has a "centripetal" force that aggregates those interests and values, and ensures that once a bargain has been reached at the apex of the political system, it will be enforced effectively.

Gerring and Thacker's theory is different from mine. One of the premises of their argument is that political preferences are endogenous to the political process. My argument treats preferences as given. Theirs is a self-avowed "grand" theory of macro-level relationships between institutions and outcomes. My theory is not. Gerring and Thacker study economic and social outcomes. I study policy choices.

But if the arguments made in Chapters 3–5 are correct, the combination of institutions that Gerring and Thacker favor should be associated with a high level of reform capacity. Parliamentarianism and a unitary state structure facilitate bargaining between different political parties since the economic and political costs of compensation are low (Chapter 3). Meanwhile, proportional elections lead to a more inclusive government, reducing the risk of potentially destructive conflicts between governments and interest groups (Chapter 4) as well as the risk of opportunistic policy reversals by future governments (Chapter 5). My findings therefore help to explain why the combination of institutions that Gerring and Thacker examine has often resulted in good government.

The third implication of this book's findings is that it is helpful to examine the origins of political compromises in power-sharing systems from a stylized rational-choice perspective. I chose such a perspective since I wished to demonstrate that power sharing is compatible with high reform capacity even if we conceive of democratic politics as the structured competition between well-defined interests, leaving no room in our models for "deliberation" and "learning." My argument about the pitfalls and promises of power sharing does not depend on a rosy view of politics.

I do not object to non-rationalistic theories of politics, such as theories of deliberative democracy (in which the preferences of political agents are endogenous to the democratic process itself). But it is useful, I think, to *start* from a rationalistic model.

In his study *Fights, Games, and Debates*, Anatol Rapoport (1960) distinguished among three types of human conflicts. In "fights," opponents try to defeat, or even destroy, one another. In "games," opponents try to dominate each other while following rules that are accepted by all. In "debates," opponents try to change each other's points of view. This book has dealt exclusively with a world of games. I have assumed that political agents have fixed preferences and self-interested motivations, and the main point that I have wished to make is that even if we make these strong assumptions about political processes, we find that it is possible for political decision-makers in power-sharing democracies to overcome democratic paralysis.

The main point of democracy, in my view, is that it transforms political conflict from a fight into a game. This is an exceptionally important achievement. Immanuel Kant wrote more than two centuries ago that the driving force of political history is the "unsocial sociability of man" (*die ungesellige Geselligkeit des Menschen*) (1991 [1784], Fourth Thesis). By choice and necessity, Kant argued, we are driven to live together in societies, but we also have competitive instincts, which drive us apart. By transforming conflict into a game—in which the underlying tension between the social and unsocial plays out according to accepted rules—democracy thus addresses the basic problem of the human condition.[1]

The hope is that with time, democracy will also turn politics from a game into a debate. But that is for another book.

## The Way We Live Now

This book has shown that in power-sharing systems, governments have used social programs and other public policies to compensate losers from reform, sheltering them from the disruptive effects of some of the major economic transformations in the twentieth and twenty-first centuries. In Chapter 2, I described, for instance, how governments have used social policy to compensate losers from trade, facilitating the liberalization of the global economy in the postwar period. I have also shown, throughout the book, that when established social programs were *themselves* reformed in the 1980s–2000s, multiparty governments, representing diverse interests, introduced more balanced reforms, compensating those who would otherwise have been harmed when unemployment benefits and pensions were adapted to the requirements of a service-based economy.

As I write this chapter, political events have once more put the question of winners and losers front and center. On June 23, 2016, a referendum in the United Kingdom resulted in a vote to leave the European Union, an outcome that was widely attributed to the unequal distribution of the gains

---

[1] Responding to a question about what we can realistically expect from democracy, Adam Przeworski once said, "Democracy is a system that keeps us from killing each other," adding that this is "good enough" (Przeworski quoted in Munck and Snyder 2007: 475). According to this minimal criterion of good government, democracy is the best form of government since it provides "a framework within which somewhat equal, somewhat effective, and somewhat free people can struggle *peacefully* to improve the world according to their different visions, values, and interests" (Przeworski 2010, 16, my emphasis). I agree with this assessment. But in addition to asking if democracy can turn politics from a "fight" into a "game," it is useful to ask if political agents are able to play the game *well*. A political system that meets Przeworski's minimal criterion has succeeded in keeping conflicts from getting completely out of hand. We can hope for a little more than that: we can try to make sure that political conflicts do not keep political decision-makers from adopting policies that are widely seen as desirable, or even necessary.

of economic openness and European integration. In the autumn of 2016, the question of international trade—which seemed to have receded into the quiet world of special-interest politics—once more became a major political issue in the United States: the Republican nominee for President, Donald Trump, made trade a top issue in the election, promising to use trade policies to protect American business and jobs.[2] Following surprise victories in states with a high proportion of white voters without a college education, such as Michigan, Ohio, Pennsylvania, and Wisconsin, Donald J. Trump went on to win the presidential election. Again, the outcome was widely attributed to the conflict between winners and losers in the modern economy.

It is not surprising that these sorts of political reactions have so far been most pronounced in majoritarian political systems such as the United Kingdom and the United States. Due to the winner-takes-all character of political competition in these countries—combined, in the case of the United States, with the failure to overcome political gridlock (see Chapter 3)—governments have arguably done less to compensate the modern economy's many losers. Governments in power-sharing systems have not always used compensation to build support for reform either (and populist, anti-immigrant parties are currently strong in many of Europe's proportional democracies). But their compensatory policies have arguably been stronger and more effective.[3]

I would like to end by identifying a potential threat to the ability of governments in power-sharing systems to overcome conflicts over reform. As I noted in Chapter 3, it has become increasingly common for national governments to delegate important policymaking competencies to international organizations, central banks, and independent agencies. The motive is simple, and in itself unobjectionable: by identifying problems that national governments have trouble solving, and handing over the management of those problems to independent decision-makers, governments hope to achieve better results within those particular areas (Majone 1998; Moravcsik 2002).

But this governance model has a downside, which is perhaps not fully appreciated in the literature. If more and more policies are delegated to independent decision-makers, the government's scope of action shrinks, and the number of policies that governments can choose from when compensating losers declines. As this book has shown, political decision-makers in power-sharing systems need room for maneuver to overcome political conflicts

---

[2] In fact, *neither* of the two candidates was unequivocally in favor of free trade, for like Donald Trump, the Democratic nominee, Hillary Clinton, opposed the free-trade agreement with the Asia-Pacific countries, the "Trans-Pacific Partnership," that President Barack Obama had pursued.

[3] Immigration, another major political issue in the advanced democracies, may be a different matter: although cross-border movements of people create winners and losers, just as cross-border movements of goods and services do, the discussion about if and how the losers from migration should be compensated is less advanced than the discussion about compensation for losers from trade, both in political discourse and among academics.

over reform. A governance model that divides public policy into separate domains, defining discrete tasks that can be delegated to experts and civil servants, makes it more difficult for governments to put together broad policy packages.

In the past, political practices in power-sharing systems were based on a very different idea about how to make democracy work: the idea that policy areas should be combined, not separated, and that conflicts are best resolved by lumping political issues together, not by splitting them. This idea seems almost quaint now, but history is long; its time might come again.

# Bibliography

Aberbach, Joel D., Robert D. Putnam, and Bert A. Rockman. 1981. *Bureaucrats and Politicians in Western Democracies*. Cambridge, MA: Harvard University Press.

Acemoglu, Daron. 2003. "Why Not a Political Coase Theorem?" *Journal of Comparative Economics* 31(4):620–52.

Acemoglu, Daron, and James A. Robinson. 2001. "Inefficient Redistribution." *American Political Science Review* 95(3):649–61.

Acemoglu, Daron, and James A. Robinson. 2006. *Economic Origins of Dictatorship and Democracy*. Cambridge, UK: Cambridge University Press.

Acemoglu, Daron, and James A. Robinson. 2012. *Why Nations Fail*. New York: Crown Business.

Adserà, Alícia, and Carles Boix. 2002. "Trade, Democracy, and the Size of the Public Sector." *International Organization* 56(2):229–62.

Aghion, Philippe, Alberto Alesina, and Francesco Trebbi. 2004. "Endogenous Political Institutions." *Quarterly Journal of Economics* 119(2):565–611.

Aidt, Toke S., and Peter S. Jensen. 2009. "The Taxman Tools Up: An Event History Study of the Introduction of the Personal Income Tax." *Journal of Public Economics* 93(1):160–75.

Aksoy, Deniz. 2012. "Institutional Arrangements and Logrolling: Evidence from the European Union." *American Journal of Political Science* 56(3):538–52.

Alesina, Alberto, and Allan Drazen. 1991. "Why Are Stabilizations Delayed?" *American Economic Review* 81(5):1170–88.

Alexiadou, Despina. 2013. "In Search of Successful Reform." *West European Politics* 36(4):704–25.

Andersen, Torben M., Michael Bergman, and Svend E. Hougaard Jensen (eds). 2015. *Reform Capacity and Macroeconomic Performance in the Nordic Countries*. Oxford: Oxford University Press.

Anderson, Karen M., and Traute Meyer. 2003. "Social Democracy, Unions, and Pension Politics in Germany and Sweden." *Journal of Public Policy* 23(1):23–54.

Andersson, Per. 2016. "The Left and Taxation: The Impact of Electoral Systems." Unpublished manuscript, Lund University.

Andersson, Per, and Johannes Lindvall. 2016. "Crises, Investments, and Institutions." Unpublished manuscript, Lund University.

Anthonsen, Mette, and Johannes Lindvall. 2009. "Party Competition and the Resilience of Corporatism." *Government and Opposition* 44(2):167–87.

Appiah, Kwame Anthony, and Martin Bunzl (eds). 2007. *Buying Freedom: The Ethics and Economics of Slave Redemption*. Princeton: Princeton University Press.

Armingeon, Klaus, Christian Isler, Laura Knöpfel, David Weisstanner, and Sarah Engler. 2016. "Comparative Political Data Set 1960–2014." Bern: Institute of Political Science, University of Berne.

Arrow, Kenneth J. 1963. *Social Choice and Individual Values*, 2nd edn. New York: Wiley.

Baccaro, Lucio, and Marco Simoni. 2008. "Policy Concertation in Europe: Understanding Government Choice." *Comparative Political Studies* 41(10):1323–48.

Bäck, Hanna, and Johannes Lindvall. 2015. "Commitment Problems in Coalitions: A New Look at the Fiscal Policies of Multiparty Governments." *Political Science Research and Methods* 3(1):53–72.

Banks, Arthur S. 2009. "Cross-National Time-Series Data Archive." Distributed by Databanks International, Jerusalem, Israel.

Bartolini, Stefano. 2000. *The Political Mobilization of the European Left, 1860–1980.* Cambridge, UK: Cambridge University Press.

Bassanini, Andrea, and Romain Duval. 2006. "The Determinants of Unemployment Across OECD Countries." *OECD Economic Studies* 42(1):7–86.

Bawn, Kathleen, and Frances Rosenbluth. 2006. "Short versus Long Coalitions: Electoral Accountability and the Size of the Public Sector." *American Journal of Political Science* 50:251–65.

Beitz, Charles R. 1989. *Political Equality*. Princeton: Princeton University Press.

Béland, Daniel, and André Lecours. 2005. "Nationalism, Public Policy, and Institutional Development: Social Security in Belgium." *Journal of Public Policy* 25(2): 265–85.

Bentham, Jeremy. 1823 [1780]. *An Introduction to the Principles of Morals and Legislation.* London: Pickering.

Beramendi, Pablo, and David Rueda. 2007. "Social Democracy Constrained: Indirect Taxation in Industrialized Democracies." *British Journal of Political Science* 37:619–41.

Bernecker, Andreas. 2014. "Divided We Reform? Evidence from US Welfare Policies." CESifo Working Paper Series 4564.

Bernhard, Michael, Timothy Nordstrom, and Christopher Reenock. 2001. "Economic Performance, Institutional Intermediation, and Democratic Survival." *Journal of Politics* 63(3):775–803.

Besley, Timothy, and Stephen Coate. 1998. "Sources of Inefficiency in a Representative Democracy." *American Economic Review* 88(1):139–56.

Besley, Timothy, and Torsten Persson. 2010. "State Capacity, Conflict, and Development." *Econometrica* 78(1):1–34.

Besley, Timothy, and Torsten Persson. 2011. *Pillars of Prosperity*. Princeton: Princeton University Press.

Binder, Sarah A. 1999. "The Dynamics of Legislative Gridlock, 1947–96." *American Political Science Review* 93(3):519–33.

Binder, Sarah A., and Frances E. Lee. 2015. "Making Deals in Congress." In *Solutions to Political Polarization in America*. Cambridge, UK: Cambridge University Press.

Birchfield, Vicki, and Markus M. L. Crepaz. 1998. "The Impact of Constitutional Structures and Collective and Competitive Veto Points on Income Inequality in Industrialized Democracies." *European Journal of Political Research* 34(2):175–200.

Blanchard, Olivier. 2006. "European Unemployment: The Evolution of Facts and Ideas." *Economic Policy* 21(45):7–59.

Bonoli, Giuliano. 1997. "Pension Politics in France: Patterns of Co-operation and Conflict in Two Recent Reforms." *West European Politics* 20(4):111–24.

Bonoli, Giuliano. 2000. *The Politics of Pension Reform*. Cambridge, UK: Cambridge University Press.

Bonoli, Giuliano. 2001. "Political Institutions, Veto Points, and the Process of Welfare State Adaptation." In *The New Politics of the Welfare State*, ed. by Paul Pierson, 238–64. Oxford: Oxford University Press.

Bonoli, Giuliano. 2013. *The Origins of Active Social Policy*. Oxford: Oxford University Press.

Brambor, Thomas. 2016. "Fiscal Capacity and the Enduring Legacy of the First Income Tax Law." Unpublished manuscript, Lund University.

Brambor, Thomas, and Johannes Lindvall. 2015. "Fiscal Capacity, Domestic Compensation, and Trade Policy: A Long-Term View." Unpublished manuscript, Lund University.

Braun, Daniela, and Swen Hutter. 2016. "Political Trust, Extrarepresentational Participation, and the Openness of Political Systems." *International Political Science Review* 37(2):151–65.

Brooks, Sarah M. 2004. "Explaining Capital Account Liberalization in Latin America." *World Politics* 56(3):389–430.

Buchanan, James M., and Gordon Tullock. 1962. *The Calculus of Consent*. Ann Arbor: University of Michigan Press.

Bueno de Mesquita, Bruce, Alastair Smith, Randolph M. Siverson, and James D. Morrow. 2003. *The Logic of Political Survival*. Cambridge, MA: MIT Press.

Burns, James MacGregor. 1963. *The Deadlock of Democracy*. Englewood Cliffs, NJ: Prentice-Hall.

Busch, Rune. 2012. "Disasters by Design: A Disaggregated Study of the Ethnic and Institutional Determinants of Natural Disaster Vulnerability." Master's thesis, University of Oslo.

Calder, K. E. 1988. *Crisis and Compensation: Public Policy and Political Stability in Japan, 1949–1986*. Princeton: Princeton University Press.

Callander, Steven, and Keith Krehbiel. 2014. "Gridlock and Delegation in a Changing World." *American Journal of Political Science* 58(4):819–34.

Calmfors, Lars, and Simon Wren-Lewis. 2011. "What Should Fiscal Councils Do?" *Economic Policy* 26(68):649–95.

Cameron, David R. 1978. "The Expansion of the Public Economy: A Comparative Analysis." *American Political Science Review* 72(4):1243–61.

Cameron, David R. 1984. "Social Democracy, Corporatism, Labour Quiescence and the Representation of Economic Interest in Advanced Capitalist Society." In *Order and Conflict in Contemporary Capitalism*, ed. by John H. Goldthorpe, 143–78. Oxford: Clarendon Press.

Cantillon, Bea, Veerle de Maesschalck, Stijn Rottiers, and Gerlinde Verbist. 2006. "Social Redistribution in Federalised Belgium." *West European Politics* 29(5): 1034–56.

Castanheira, Micael, Vincenzo Galasso, Stéphane Carcillo, Giuseppe Nicoletti, Enrico Perotti, and Lidia Tsyganok. 2006. "How to Gain Political Support for Reforms." In *Structural Reforms Without Prejudices*, ed. by Tito Boeri, Micael Castanheira, Riccardo Faini, and Vincenzo Galasso, 141–202. Oxford: Oxford University Press.

Castro, Rui, and Daniele Coen-Pirani. 2003. "Compensations as Signaling Devices in the Political Economy of Reforms." *International Economic Review* 44(3):1061–78.

Cheibub, José Antonio, Adam Przeworski, and Sebastian M. Saiegh. 2004. "Government Coalitions and Legislative Success under Presidentialism and Parliamentarism." *British Journal of Political Science* 34(4):565–87.

Clarke, James Freeman. 1870. "Wanted, a Statesman!" *Old and New Magazine* 2(6):644–50.

Clemens, Michael A., and Jeffrey G. Williamson. 2004. "Why Did the Tariff-Growth Correlation Change after 1950?" *Journal of Economic Growth* 9(1):5–46.

Coase, Ronald H. 1960. "The Problem of Social Cost." *Journal of Law and Economics* 3(October):1–44.

Cohen, Charles, and Eric D. Werker. 2008. "The Political Economy of 'Natural' Disasters." *Journal of Conflict Resolution* 52(6):795–819.

Cox, Gary W., and Mathew D. McCubbins. 2001. "The Institutional Determinants of Economic Policy Outcomes." In *Presidents, Parliaments, and Policy*, ed. by Stephan Haggard and Mathew D. McCubbins, 21–63. Cambridge, UK: Cambridge University Press.

Cox, Robert H. 2001. "The Social Construction of an Imperative." *World Politics* 53(3):463–98.

Crepaz, Markus M. L. 1996. "Constitutional Structures and Regime Performance in 18 Industrialized Democracies." *European Journal of Political Research* 29(1):87–104.

Crepaz, Markus M. L. 1998. "Inclusion versus Exclusion: Political Institutions and Welfare Expenditures." *Comparative Politics* 31(1):61–80.

Crozier, Michael, Samuel P. Huntington, and Joji Watanuki. 1975. *The Crisis of Democracy: Report on the Governability of Democracies to the Trilateral Commission*. New York: New York University Press.

Cukierman, Alex. 1992. *Central Bank Strategy, Credibility, and Independence*. Cambridge, MA: MIT Press.

Culpepper, Pepper D. 2002. "Powering, Puzzling, and 'Pacting': The Informational Logic of Negotiated Reforms." *Journal of European Public Policy* 9(5):774–90.

Dahl, Robert A. 1957. "Decision-Making in a Democracy: The Supreme Court as a National Policy-Maker." *Journal of Public Law* 6:279–95.

Dahlström, Carl, Victor Lapuente, and Jan Teorell. 2012. "The Merit of Meritocratization." *Political Research Quarterly* 65(3):656–68.

Dahlström, Carl, Johannes Lindvall, and Bo Rothstein. 2013. "Corruption, Bureaucratic Failure and Social Policy Priorities." *Political Studies* 61(3):523–42.

Davidson, Carl, and Steven J. Matusz. 2006. "Trade Liberalization and Compensation." *International Economic Review* 47(3):723–47.

Davidsson, Johan Bo, and Patrick Emmenegger. 2013. "Defending the Organisation, Not the Members: Unions and the Reform of Job Security Legislation in Western Europe." *European Journal of Political Research* 52(3):339–63.

de Deken, Johan. 2007. "Distribution of Responsibility for Social Security and Labour Market Policy. Country Report: Belgium." AIAS working paper 2007–53, Amsterdam: University of Amsterdam.

de Figueiredo Jr., Rui J. P. 2002. "Electoral Competition, Political Uncertainty, and Policy Insulation." *American Political Science Review* 96(2):321–33.

de Haan, Jakob, and Jan-Egbert Sturm. 1997. "Political and Economic Determinants of OECD Budget Deficits and Government Expenditures: A Reinvestigation." *European Journal of Political Economy* 13(4):739–50.

de Haan, Jakob, Jan-Egbert Sturm, and Geert Beekhuis. 1999. "The Weak Government Thesis: Some New Evidence." *Public Choice* 101(3):163–76.

Diamond, Larry J. 1990. "Three Paradoxes of Democracy." *Journal of Democracy* 1(3):48–60.

Dingeldey, Irene. 2007. "Between Workfare and Enablement—The Different Paths to Transformation of the Welfare State." *European Journal of Political Research* 46(6): 823–51.

Dixit, Avinash. 1996. *The Making of Economic Policy*. Cambridge, MA: MIT Press.

Dixit, Avinash, Gene M. Grossman, and Faruk Gul. 2000. "The Dynamics of Political Compromise." *Journal of Political Economy* 108(3):531–68.

Dixit, Avinash, and John Londregan. 1995. "Redistributive Politics and Economic Efficiency." *American Political Science Review* 89(4):856–66.

Dixit, Avinash, and Victor Norman. 1986. "Gains from Trade without Lump-Sum Compensation." *Journal of International Economics* 21(1–2):111–22.

Domenach, Jean-Marie. 1958. "Democratic Paralysis in France." *Foreign Affairs* 37(1):31–44.

Downs, Anthony. 1957. *An Economic Theory of Democracy*. New York: Harper & Row.

Drazen, Allan. 2000. *Political Economy in Macroeconomics*. Princeton: Princeton University Press.

Drazen, Allan, and Vittorio Grilli. 1993. "The Benefit of Crisis for Economic Reform." *American Economic Review* 83(2):588–608.

Duval, Romain, and Jørgen Elmeskov. 2005. "The Effects of EMU on Structural Reforms in Labour and Product Markets." OECD Economics Department Working Paper 438.

Dyson, Kenneth, and Angelos Sepos. 2010. "Differentiation as Design Principle and as Tool in the Political Management of European Integration." In *Which Europe?*, ed. by Kenneth Dyson and Angelos Sepos, 3–23. Basingstoke: Palgrave Macmillan.

Ebbinghaus, Bernhard. 2006. *Reforming Early Retirement in Europe, Japan, and the USA*. Oxford: Oxford University Press.

Edin, Per-Anders, and Henry Ohlsson. 1991. "Political Determinants of Budget Deficits: Coalition Effects versus Minority Effects." *European Economic Review* 35(8):1597–603.

Ehrenhalt, Alan. 1982. "The Individualist Senate." *Congressional Quarterly Weekly Report*, September 4, 1982, 2175–82.

Eichhorst, Werner, Otto Kaufmann, Regina Konle-Seidl, and Hans-Joachim Reinhard. 2008. "Bringing the Jobless into Work?" In *Bringing the Jobless into Work?*, ed. by Werner Eichhorst, Otto Kaufmann, and Regina Konle-Seidl, 1–16. Berlin: Springer.

Eisinger, Peter K. 1973. "The Conditions of Protest Behavior in American Cities." *American Political Science Review* 67(1):11–28.

Ellman, Matthew, and Leonard Wantchekon. 2000. "Electoral Competition under the Threat of Political Unrest." *Quarterly Journal of Economics* 115(2):499–531.

Elster, Jon (ed.) 1998. *Deliberative Democracy*. Cambridge, UK: Cambridge University Press.

Emmenegger, Patrick. 2014. *The Power to Dismiss*. Oxford: Oxford University Press.

Etchemendy, Sebastián. 2001. "Constructing Reform Coalitions: The Politics of Compensations in Argentina's Economic Liberalization." *Latin American Politics and Society* 43(3):1–36.

Etchemendy, Sebastián. 2011. *Models of Economic Liberalization*. Cambridge, UK: Cambridge University Press.

Evans, Diana. 1994. "Policy and Pork: The Use of Pork Barrel Projects to Build Policy Coalitions in the House of Representatives." *American Journal of Political Science* 38(4):894–917.

Faniel, Jean. 2005. "Réactions syndicales et associatives face au 'contrôle de la disponibilité des chômeurs'." *Année sociale 2004*:133–48.

Fearon, James. 1994. "Domestic Political Audiences and the Escalation of International Disputes." *American Political Science Review* 88(3):577–92.

Fearon, James. 1995. "Rationalist Explanations for War." *International Organization* 49(3):379–414.

Fearon, James. 2004. "Why Do Some Civil Wars Last So Much Longer Than Others?" *Journal of Peace Research* 41(3):275–301.

Featherstone, Kevin, and Dimitris Papadimitriou. 2008. *The Limits of Europeanization: Reform Capacity and Policy Conflict in Greece*. Basingstoke: Palgrave.

Fernandez, Raquel, and Dani Rodrik. 1991. "Resistance to Reform: Status Quo Bias in the Presence of Individual-Specific Uncertainty." *American Economic Review* 81(5):1146–55.

Fernández-Albertos, José, and Víctor Lapuente. 2011. "Doomed to Disagree? Party-Voter Discipline and Policy Gridlock Under Divided Government." *Party Politics* 17(6):801–22.

Fillieule, Olivier. 1997. *Strategies de la rue*. Paris: Presses de Sciences Po.

Finer, Herman. 1924. *The Case Against Proportional Representation*. London: Fabian Society.

Finer, Herman. 1935. *The Case Against Proportional Representation*, 2nd edn. London: Fabian Society.

Finer, Samuel E. 1997. *The History of Government*, 3 vols. Oxford: Oxford University Press.

Fladeland, Betty L. 1976. "Compensated Emancipation: A Rejected Alternative." *Journal of Southern History* 42(2):169–86.

Flora, Peter, Franz Kraus, and Winfried Pfenning. 1983. *State, Economy, and Society in Western Europe 1815–1975: The Growth of Industrial Societies and Capitalist Economies*. Frankfurt: Campus Verlag.

Fondazione Rodolfo Debenedetti. 2010. "The fRDB-IZA Social Reforms Database." Milan: Fondazione Rodolfo Debenedetti.

Franzese, Jr., Robert J. 2002. *Macroeconomic Policies of Developed Democracies.* Cambridge, UK: Cambridge University Press.

Fredriksson, Peter, and Bertil Holmlund. 2006. "Improving Incentives in Unemployment Insurance." *Journal of Economic Surveys* 20(3):357–86.

Freyssinet, Jacques. 2007. "L'accord du 11 janvier 2008 sur la modernisation du marché du travail." *Revue de l'IRES* 54(2):3–39.

Gehlbach, Scott, and Edmund J. Malesky. 2010. "The Contribution of Veto Players to Economic Reform." *Journal of Politics* 72(4):957–75.

Gerring, John, and Strom C. Thacker. 2010. *Centripetal Democratic Governance.* Cambridge, UK: Cambridge University Press.

Giger, Natalie, and Moira Nelson. 2013. "The Welfare State or the Economy? Preferences, Constituencies, and Strategies for Retrenchment." *European Sociological Review* 29(5):1083–94.

Granovetter, Mark S. 1973. "The Strength of Weak Ties." *American Journal of Sociology* 78(6):1360–80.

Grant, Wyn. 2000. *Pressure Groups and British Politics.* Basingstoke: Macmillan.

Groseclose, Tim, and Nolan McCarty. 2001. "The Politics of Blame: Bargaining before an Audience." *American Journal of Political Science* 45(1):100–19.

Gutmann, Amy, and Dennis Thompson. 2012. *The Spirit of Compromise.* Princeton: Princeton University Press.

Hacker, Jacob S., and Paul Pierson. 2010. *Winner-Take-All Politics.* New York: Simon and Schuster.

Hall, Peter, and Michelle Lamont. 2009. *Successful Societies.* Cambridge, UK: Cambridge University Press.

Hallerberg, Mark. 2004. *Domestic Budgets in a United Europe.* Ithaca, NY: Cornell University Press.

Hallerberg, Mark, and Scott Basinger. 1998. "Internationalization and Changes in Tax Policy in OECD Countries: The Importance of Domestic Veto Players." *Comparative Political Studies* 31(3):321–52.

Hallerberg, Mark, and Jürgen von Hagen. 1999. "Electoral Institutions, Cabinet Negotiations, and Budget Deficits within the European Union." In *Fiscal Institutions and Fiscal Performance*, ed. by James M. Poterba and Jürgen von Hagen, 209–32. Chicago: University of Chicago Press.

Hamann, Kerstin, and John Kelly. 2007. "Party Politics and the Reemergence of Social Pacts in Western Europe." *Comparative Political Studies* 40(8):971–94.

Hamilton, Alexander. 2003 [1787]. "Federalist No. 1." In *The Federalist*, 1–4. Cambridge, UK: Cambridge University Press.

Häusermann, Silja. 2010. *The Politics of Welfare State Reform in Continental Europe.* Cambridge, UK: Cambridge University Press.

Hays, Jude C., Sean D. Ehrlich, and Clint Peinhardt. 2005. "Government Spending and Public Support for Trade in the OECD." *International Organization* 59(2):473–94.

Heclo, Hugh. 1974. *Modern Social Policies in Britain and Sweden.* New Haven: Yale University Press.

Hellman, Joel. 1998. "Winners Take All: The Politics of Partial Reform in Postcommunist Transitions." *World Politics* 50(2):203–34.

Hemerijck, Anton. 1992. "The Historical Contingencies of Dutch Corporatism." Ph.D. thesis, University of Oxford.

Hemerijck, Anton C., and Martin Schludi. 2000. "Sequences of Policy Failures and Effective Policy Responses." In *Welfare and Work in the Open Economy*, Vol. I, ed. by Fritz W. Scharpf and Vivien A. Schmidt, 125–228. Oxford: Oxford University Press.

Hemerijck, Anton C., Birgitte Unger, and Jelle Visser. 2000. "How Small Countries Negotiate Change." In *Welfare and Work in the Open Economy*, Vol. II, ed. by Fritz W. Scharpf and Vivien A. Schmidt, 175–263. Oxford: Oxford University Press.

Henisz, Witold J. 2000. "The Institutional Environment for Economic Growth." *Economics & Politics* 12(1):1–31.

Henisz, Witold J. 2004. "Political Institutions and Policy Volatility." *Economics & Politics* 16(1):1–27.

Héritier, Adrienne. 1999. *Policy-Making and Diversity in Europe*. Cambridge, UK: Cambridge University Press.

Hermens, Ferdinand A. 1941. *Democracy or Anarchy?* Notre Dame: University of Notre Dame.

Hermens, Ferdinand A. 1972. *Democracy or Anarchy?* 2nd edn. New York: Johnson Reprint.

Hessami, Zohal. 2016. "How Do Voters React to Complex Choices in a Direct Democracy? Evidence from Switzerland." *Kyklos* 69(2):263–93.

Hibbs, Douglas A. 1978. "On the Political Economy of Long-Run Trends in Strike Activity." *British Journal of Political Science* 8(2):153–75.

Hicks, John. 1939. "The Foundations of Welfare Economics." *Economic Journal* 49(196):696–712.

Hicks, John. 1963 [1932]. *The Theory of Wages*, 2nd edn. London: Macmillan.

Hix, Simon, and Bjørn Høyland. 2011. *The Political System of the European Union*, 3rd edn. Basingstoke: Palgrave Macmillan.

Hoffmann, Stanley. 1963. "Paradoxes of the French Political Community." In *In Search of France*, ed. by Stanley Hoffman, 1–117. Cambridge, MA: Center for International Affairs, Harvard University.

Hopmann, P. Terrence. 1996. *The Negotiation Process and the Resolution of International Conflicts*. Columbia: University of South Carolina Press.

Howard, Dick. 1998. "The French Strikes of 1995 and their Political Aftermath." *Government and Opposition* 33(2):199–220.

Huber, Evelyne, and Juan Bogliaccini. 2010. "Latin America." In *The Oxford Handbook of the Welfare State*, ed. by Francis G. Castles, Stephan Leibfried, Jane Lewis, Herbert Obinger, and Christopher Pierson. Oxford: Oxford University Press.

Huber, Evelyne, Charles Ragin, and John D. Stephens. 1993. "Social Democracy, Christian Democracy, Constitutional Structure, and the Welfare State." *American Journal of Sociology* 99(3):711–49.

Hutter, Swen. 2014. *Protesting Culture and Economics in Western Europe*. Minneapolis: University of Minnesota Press.

ILO. 1956. *Social Aspects of European Economic Co-operation*. Geneva: International Labour Office.

Immergut, Ellen M. 1992. *Health Politics*. Cambridge, UK: Cambridge University Press.

Immergut, Ellen M., and Karen M. Anderson. 2007. "Editors' Introduction: The Dynamics of Pension Politics." In *The Handbook of West European Pension Politics*, ed. by Ellen M. Immergut, Karen M. Anderson, and Isabelle Schulze, 1–17. Oxford: Oxford University Press.

Immergut, Ellen M., Karen M. Anderson, and Isabelle Schulze (eds). 2007. *The Handbook of West European Pension Politics*. Oxford: Oxford University Press.

Iversen, Torben, and David Soskice. 2015. "Democratic Limits to Redistribution: Inclusionary versus Exclusionary Coalitions in the Knowledge Economy." *World Politics* 67(2):185–225.

Jacobs, Alan M. 2011. *Governing for the Long Term: Democracy and the Politics of Investment*. Cambridge, UK: Cambridge University Press.

Jacobs, Alan M. 2016. "Policy Making for the Long Term in Advanced Democracies." *Annual Review of Political Science* 19:433–54.

Jordana, Jacint, David Levi-Faur, and Xavier Fernández i Marín. 2011. "The Global Diffusion of Regulatory Agencies." *Comparative Political Studies* 44(10):1343–69.

Kaldor, Nicholas. 1939. "Welfare Propositions of Economics and Interpersonal Comparisons of Utility." *Economic Journal* 49(195):549–52.

Kant, Immanuel. 1991 [1784]. "Idea for a Universal History with Cosmopolitan Purpose." In *Political Writings*, 41–53. Cambridge, UK: Cambridge University Press.

Kardasheva, Raya. 2013. "Package Deals in EU Legislative Politics." *American Journal of Political Science* 57(4):858–74.

Katzenstein, Peter J. 1985. *Small States in World Markets*. Ithaca, NY: Cornell University Press.

Keeler, John T. S. 1993a. "Executive Power and Policymaking Patterns in France: Gauging the Impact of Fifth Republic Institutions." *West European Politics* 16(4): 518–44.

Keeler, John T. S. 1993b. "Opening the Window For Reform." *Comparative Political Studies* 25(4):433–86.

Kellow, Margaret M. R. 2007. "Conflicting Imperatives: Black and White American Abolitionists Debate Slave Redemption." In *Buying Freedom*, ed. by Kwame Anthony Appiah and Martin Bunzl, 200–22. Princeton: Princeton University Press.

Kelly, John, Kerstin Hamann, and Alison Johnston. 2013. "Unions Against Governments: Explaining General Strikes in Western Europe, 1980–2006." *Comparative Political Studies* 46(9):1030–57.

Kenner, Jeff. 2003. *EU Employment Law*. Oxford: Hart Publishing.

Kirkland, Justin H. 2011. "The Relational Determinants of Legislative Outcomes." *Journal of Politics* 73(3):887–98.

Knotz, Carlo, and Johannes Lindvall. 2015. "Coalitions and Compensation: The Case of Unemployment Benefit Duration." *Comparative Political Studies* 48(5): 586–615.

König, Thomas, Marc Debus, and George Tsebelis (eds). 2010. *Reform Processes and Policy Change*. New York: Springer.

König, Thomas and Dirk Junge. 2010. "Why Don't Veto Players Use Their Power?" In *Reform Processes and Policy Change*, ed. by Thomas König, George Tsebelis, and Marc Debus, 165–86. New York: Springer.

149

Korpi, Walter, and Joakim Palme. 2008. *The Social Citizenship Indicator Program (SCIP)*. Swedish Institute for Social Research.

Korpi, Walter, and Michael Shalev. 1979. "Strikes, Industrial Relations and Class Conflict in Industrial Societies." *British Journal of Sociology* 30(2):164–87.

Kriesi, Hanspeter, Ruud Koopmans, Jan Willem Duyvendak, and Marco G. Giugni. 1995. *New Social Movements in Western Europe*. London: UCL Press.

Krusell, Per, and José-Víctor Ríos-Rull. 1996. "Vested Interests in a Positive Theory of Stagnation and Growth." *Review of Economic Studies* 63(2):301–29.

Kurtz, Marcus J., and Sarah M. Brooks. 2008. "Embedding Neoliberal Reform in Latin America." *World Politics* 60(2):231–80.

Ladner, Andreas. 2004. "The Political Parties and the Party System." In *Handbook of Swiss Politics*, ed. by Ulrich Klöti, Peter Knoepfel, Hanspeter Kriesi, Wolf Linder, and Yannis Papadopoulos. Zurich: Neue Zürcher Zeitung Verlag.

Lamothe, P. 2006. "Comprendre le changement comme un processus de discussion. L'exemple de la réforme des retraites 2003." *Revue française de science politique* 56(4):593–617.

Lampe, Markus, and Paul Sharp. 2013. "Tariffs and Income: A Time Series Analysis for 24 Countries." *Cliometrica* 7(3):207–35.

Laver, Michael, and Kenneth A. Shepsle. 1991. "Divided Government: America is Not 'Exceptional'." *Governance* 4(3):250–69.

Lax, David A., and James K. Sebenius. 1986. *The Manager as Negotiator*. New York: Free Press.

Layard, Richard, Stephen Nickell, and Richard Jackman. 1991. *Unemployment*. Oxford: Oxford University Press.

Layard, Richard, Stephen Nickell, and Richard Jackman. 1994. *The Unemployment Crisis*. Oxford: Oxford University Press.

Lijphart, Arend. 1968. *The Politics of Accommodation*. Berkeley: University of California Press.

Lijphart, Arend. 1977. "Majority Rule versus Democracy in Deeply Divided Societies." *Politikon* 4(2):113–26.

Lijphart, Arend. 1984. *Democracies*. New Haven: Yale University Press.

Lijphart, Arend. 1999. *Patterns of Democracy*. New Haven: Yale University Press.

Lijphart, Arend. 2012. *Patterns of Democracy*, 2nd edn. New Haven: Yale University Press.

Lijphart, Arend, and Markus M. L. Crepaz. 1991. "Corporatism and Consensus Democracy in Eighteen Countries." *British Journal of Political Science* 21(1):235–46.

Lindblom, Charles E. 1977. *Politics and Markets*. New York: Basic Books.

Lindblom, Charles E. 1982. "The Market as Prison." *Journal of Politics* 44(2):324–36.

Lindvall, Johannes. 2010a. *Mass Unemployment and the State*. Oxford: Oxford University Press.

Lindvall, Johannes. 2010b. "Power Sharing and Reform Capacity." *Journal of Theoretical Politics* 22(3):1–18.

Lindvall, Johannes. 2011. "The Political Foundations of Trust and Distrust: Reforms and Protests in France." *West European Politics* 34(2):296–316.

Lindvall, Johannes. 2012. "Politics and Policies in Two Economic Crises: The Nordic Countries." In *Coping With Crisis*, ed. by Nancy Bermeo and Jonas Pontusson, 233–60. New York: Russell Sage Foundation.

Lindvall, Johannes. 2013. "Union Density and Political Strikes." *World Politics* 65(3):539–69.

Lindvall, Johannes, and Joakim Sebring. 2005. "Policy Reform and the Decline of Swedish Corporatism." *West European Politics* 28(5):1057–74.

Linz, Juan J. 1998. "Democracy's Time Constraints." *International Political Science Review* 19(1):19–37.

Lipsky, Michael. 1968. "Protest as a Political Resource." *American Political Science Review* 62(4):1144–58.

Lowell, A. Lawrence. 1896. *Governments and Parties in Continental Europe*. London: Longmans, Green.

McAdam, Doug. 1999 [1982]. *Political Process and the Development of Black Insurgency 1930–1970*, 2nd edn. Chicago: University of Chicago Press.

McAdam, Doug, Sidney Tarrow, and Charles Tilly. 2001. *Dynamics of Contention*. Cambridge, UK: Cambridge University Press.

McCarty, Nolan. 2000. "Proposal Rights, Veto Rights, and Political Bargaining." *American Journal of Political Science* 44(3):506–22.

McCarty, Nolan, Keith T. Poole, and Howard Rosenthal. 2016. *Polarized America*, 2nd edn. Cambridge, MA: MIT Press.

McGann, Anthony J., and Michael Latner. 2013. "The Calculus of Consensus Democracy." *Comparative Political Studies* 46(7):823–50.

Mach, André. 2004. "Interest Groups." In *Handbook of Swiss Politics*, ed. by Ulrich Klöti, Peter Knoepfel, Hanspeter Kriesi, Wolf Linder, and Yannis Papadopoulos, 279–313. Zürich: Neue Zürcher Zeitung Verlag.

Machado, Fabiana, Carlos Scartascini, and Mariano Tommasi. 2011. "Political Institutions and Street Protests in Latin America." *Journal of Conflict Resolution* 55(3): 340–65.

MacIntyre, Andrew. 2001. "Institutions and Investors: The Politics of the Economic Crisis in Southeast Asia." *International Organization* 55(1):81–122.

McLean, Iain, and Alistair McMillan. 2015. *The Concise Oxford Dictionary of Politics*, 3rd edn. Oxford University Press.

Majone, Giandomenico. 1998. "Europe's 'Democratic Deficit'." *European Law Journal* 4(1):5–28.

Mansbridge, Jane. 2012. "On the Importance of Getting Things Done." *PS: Political Science & Politics* 45(1):1–8.

Mansbridge, Jane, and Cathie Jo Martin (eds). 2013. *Negotiating Agreement in Politics*. Washington, DC: American Political Science Association.

Mares, Isabela. 2004. "Economic Insecurity and Social Policy Expansion: Evidence from Interwar Europe." *International Organization* 58(4):745–74.

Mares, Isabela, and Didac Queralt. 2015. "The Non-Democratic Origins of Income Taxation." *Comparative Political Studies* 48(14):1974–2009.

Margalit, Avishai. 2010. *On Compromise and Rotten Compromises*. Princeton: Princeton University Press.

Martin, Cathie Jo. 2004. "Reinventing Welfare Regimes." *World Politics* 57(1):39–69.

Martin, Cathie Jo, and Duane Swank. 2008. "The Political Origins of Coordinated Capitalism." *American Political Science Review* 102(2):181–98.

Martin, Cathie Jo, and Duane Swank. 2011. "Gonna Party Like It's 1899: Party Systems and the Origins of Varieties of Coordination." *World Politics* 63(1):78–114.

Martin, Lanny W., and Georg Vanberg. 2004. "Policing the Bargain: Coalition Government and Parliamentary Scrutiny." *American Journal of Political Science* 48(1): 13–27.

Martin, Lanny W., and Georg Vanberg. 2011. *Parliaments and Coalitions*. Oxford: Oxford University Press.

Martin, Lisa L. 2000. *Democratic Commitments*. Princeton: Princeton University Press.

Mayhew, David R. 1991. *Divided We Govern*. New Haven: Yale University Press.

Mejía Acosta, Andrés. 2009. *Informal Coalitions and Policymaking in Latin America*. London: Routledge.

Milward, Alan S. 1992. *The European Rescue of the Nation-State*. London: Routledge.

Mitchell, Matthew F. and Andrea Moro. 2006. "Persistent Distortionary Policies with Asymmetric Information." *American Economic Review* 96(1):387–93.

Moe, Terry M. 1990. "The Politics of Structural Choice: Towards a Theory of Public Bureaucracy." In *Organization Theory*, ed. Oliver E. Williamson, 116–53. Berkeley: University of California Press.

Moe, Terry M., and Michael Caldwell. 1994. "The Institutional Foundations of Democratic Government." *Journal of Institutional and Theoretical Economics* 150(1):171–95.

Moravcsik, Andrew. 1999. *The Choice for Europe*. Ithaca, NY: Cornell University Press.

Moravcsik, Andrew. 2002. "Reassessing Legitimacy in the European Union." *Journal of Common Market Studies* 40(4):603–24.

Mukherjee, Bumba, and David Andrew Singer. 2010. "International Institutions and Domestic Compensation: The IMF and the Politics of Capital Account Liberalization." *American Journal of Political Science* 54(1):45–60.

Muller, Clemma J., and Richard F. MacLehose. 2014. "Estimating Predicted Probabilities from Logistic Regression." *International Journal of Epidemiology* 43(3):962–70.

Müller, Wolfgang C., and Kaare Strøm. 2003. "Coalition Governance in Western Europe." In *Coalition Government in Western Europe*, ed. Kaare Strøm and Wolfgang C. Müller, 1–31. Oxford: Oxford University Press.

Munck, Gerardo L., and Richard Snyder. 2007. *Passion, Craft, and Method in Comparative Politics*. Baltimore: Johns Hopkins University Press.

Murillo, Maria Victoria. 2000. "From Populism to Neoliberalism: Labor Unions and Market Reforms in Latin America." *World Politics* 52(2):135–74.

Murillo, Maria Victoria. 2001. *Labor Unions, Partisan Coalitions, and Market Reforms in Latin America*. Cambridge, UK: Cambridge University Press.

Nam, Taehyun. 2007. "Rough Days in Democracies: Comparing Protests in Democracies." *European Journal of Political Research* 46(1):97–120.

Naurin, Daniel. 2007. *Deliberation Behind Closed Doors*. Colchester: ECPR Press.

Nickell, Stephen, and Richard Layard. 1999. "Labor Market Institutions and Economic Performance." In *Handbook of Labor Economics*, ed. by Orley Ashenfelter and David Card, 3030–84. New York: Elsevier.

Nooruddin, Irfan. 2011. *Coalition Politics and Economic Development*. Cambridge, UK: Cambridge University Press.

North, Douglass C. 1990. *Institutions, Institutional Change, and Economic Performance*. Cambridge, UK: Cambridge University Press.

North, Douglass C., and Robert Paul Thomas. 1973. *The Rise of the Western World*. Cambridge, UK: Cambridge University Press.

OECD. 1999. *Implementing the OECD Jobs Strategy*. Paris: OECD.

OECD. 2007. *Economic Survey: Belgium*. Paris: OECD.

*Oxford English Dictionary*. 2016. "OED Online." Last accessed in September 2016.

Palier, Bruno. 2005. *Gouverner la sécurité sociale*. Paris: Presses Universitaires de France.

Persson, Torsten. 2005. "Forms of Democracy, Policy and Economic Development." Unpublished manuscript, Stockholm University.

Persson, Torsten, Gerard Roland, and Guido Tabellini. 2007. "Electoral Rules and Government Spending in Parliamentary Democracies." *Quarterly Journal of Political Science* 2(2):155–88.

Persson, Torsten, and Guido Tabellini. 2003. *The Economic Effects of Constitutions*. Cambridge, MA: MIT Press.

Persson, Torsten, and Guido Tabellini. 2006. "Electoral Systems and Economic Policy." In *The Oxford Handbook of Political Economy*, ed. Barry R. Weingast and Donald A. Wittman, 723–36. Oxford: Oxford University Press.

Persson, Torsten, and Guido Tabellini. 2009. "Democratic Capital." *American Economic Journal: Macroeconomics* 1(2):88–126.

Pierson, Paul. 2001. "Coping With Permanent Austerity." In *The New Politics of the Welfare State*, ed. Paul Pierson, 410–56. Oxford: Oxford University Press.

Pierson, Paul, and R. Kent Weaver. 1993. "Imposing Losses in Pension Policy." In *Do Institutions Matter?*, ed. R. Kent Weaver and Bert A. Rockman, 110–50. Washington, DC: Brookings Institution.

Powell, G. Bingham. 2000. *Elections as Instruments of Democracy*. New Haven: Yale University Press.

Powell, Robert. 2004. "The Inefficient Use of Power." *American Political Science Review* 98(2):231–41.

Pruitt, Dean G. 1981. *Negotiation Behavior*. New York: Academic Press.

Przeworski, Adam. 2010. *Democracy and the Limits of Self-Government*. Cambridge, UK: Cambridge University Press.

Przeworski, Adam, Susan C. Stokes, and Bernard Manin. 1999. *Democracy, Accountability, and Representation*. Cambridge, UK: Cambridge University Press.

Rapoport, Anatol. 1960. *Fights, Games, and Debates*. Ann Arbor: University of Michigan Press.

Rawls, John. 1971. *A Theory of Justice*. Cambridge, MA: Harvard University Press.

Rawls, John. 1993. *Political Liberalism*. New York: Columbia University Press.

Ricardo, David. 1817. *On the Principles of Political Economy and Taxation*. London: John Murray.

Rieselbach, Leroy N. 1994. *Congressional Reform*. Washington, DC: CQ Press.

Riker, William H. 1962. *The Theory of Political Coalitions*. New Haven: Yale University Press.

Riker, William H. 1975. "Federalism." In *Handbook of Political Science*, Vol. 5, ed. by Fred Greenstein and Nelson Polsby, 93–172. Reading, MA: Addison-Wesley.

Riker, William H. 1984. "Duverger's Law Revisited." In *Electoral Laws and Their Political Consequences*, ed. Bernard Grofman and Arend Lijphart, 19–42. New York: Agathon Press.

Robinson, James A., and Daron Acemoglu. 2006. "De Facto Political Power and Institutional Persistence." *American Economic Review* 96(2):326–30.

Rodrik, Dani. 1994. "The Rush to Free Trade in the Developing World: Why So Late? Why Now? Will it Last?" In *Voting for Reform*, ed. Stephen Haggard and Steven B. Webb, 61–88. Washington, DC: World Bank Publications.

Rodrik, Dani. 1998. "Why Do More Open Economies Have Bigger Governments?" *Journal of Political Economy* 106(5):997–1032.

Roemer, John E. 2001. *Political Competition*. Cambridge, MA: Harvard University Press.

Rogowski, Ronald. 1987. "Trade and the Variety of Democratic Institutions." *International Organization* 41(2):203–23.

Roller, Edeltraud. 2005. *The Performance of Democracies*. Oxford: Oxford University Press.

Rose, Richard. 1979. "Ungovernability: Is There Fire Beneath the Smoke?" *Political Studies* 27(3):351–70.

Rose-Ackerman, Rose. 1999. *Corruption and Government*. Cambridge, UK: Cambridge University Press.

Ross, Lee, and Andrew Ward. 1995. "Psychological Barriers to Dispute Resolution." *Advances in Experimental Social Psychology* 27:255–304.

Rothstein, Bo. 1992. *Den korporativa staten*. Stockholm: Norstedts.

Rothstein, Bo. 2011. *The Quality of Government*. Chicago: University of Chicago Press.

Rothstein, Bo, and Jan Teorell. 2008. "What Is Quality of Government?" *Governance* 21(2):165–90.

Roubini, Nouriel, and Jeffrey Sachs. 1989. "Political and Economic Determinants of Budget Deficits in the Industrial Democracies." *European Economic Review* 33(5): 903–38.

Ruggie, John G. 1982. "International Regimes, Transactions, and Change: Embedded Liberalism in the Postwar Economic Order." *International Organization* 36(2): 379–415.

Ryan, Timothy J. 2016. "No Compromise: Political Consequences of Moralized Attitudes." *American Journal of Political Science*. DOI:10.111/ajps.12248.

Safire, William. 1993. *Safire's New Political Dictionary*. New York: Random House.

Samuels, David. 2003. *Ambition, Federalism, and Legislative Politics in Brazil*. Cambridge, UK: Cambridge University Press.

Sartori, Giovanni. 1987. *The Theory of Democracy Revisited*. Chatham, NJ: Chatham House.

Sartori, Giovanni. 1997. *Comparative Constitutional Engineering*, 2nd edn. Houndmills: Palgrave.

Scartascini, Carlos, and Mariano Tommasi. 2012. "The Making of Policy: Institutionalized or Not?" *American Journal of Political Science* 4(4):787–801.

Schelling, Thomas C. 1956. "An Essay on Bargaining." *American Economic Review* 46(3):281–306.

Schludi, Martin. 2005. *The Reform of Bismarckian Pension Systems*. Amsterdam: Amsterdam University Press.

Schmidt, Manfred G. 2002. "Political Performance and Types of Democracy: Findings from Comparative Studies." *European Journal of Political Research* 41(1):147–63.

Schumpeter, Joseph A. 1942. *Capitalism, Socialism, and Democracy*. New York: Harper & Brothers.

Scitovszky, Tibor De. 1941. "A Note on Welfare Propositions in Economics." *Review of Economic Studies* 9(1):77–88.

Scruggs, Lyle and James Allan. 2006. "Welfare-State Decommodification in 18 OECD Countries." *Journal of European Social Policy* 16(1):55–72.

Segal, Jeffrey A., and Harold J. Spaeth. 2002. *The Supreme Court and the Attitudinal Model Revisited*. Cambridge, UK: Cambridge University Press.

Smith, Adam. 1776. *An Inquiry into the Nature and Causes of the Wealth of Nations*. London: W. Strahan and T. Cadell.

Sol, Els, Markus Sichert, Harm van Lieshout, and Theo Koning. 2008. "Activation as a Socio-Economic and Legal Concept: Laboratorium the Netherlands." In *Bringing the Jobless into Work?*, ed. Werner Eichhorst, Otto Kaufmann, and Regina Konle-Seidl, 161–220. Berlin: Springer.

Spiller, Pablo T., and Mariano Tommasi. 2009. *The Institutional Foundations of Public Policy in Argentina*. Cambridge, UK: Cambridge University Press.

Stein, Ernesto, and Mariano Tommasi (eds). 2008. *Policymaking in Latin America: How Politics Shapes Policies*. Washington, DC: Inter-American Development Bank.

Steinmo, Sven. 1993. *Taxation and Democracy*. New Haven: Yale University Press.

Stolper, Wolfgang F., and Paul A. Samuelson. 1941. "Protection and Real Wages." *Review of Economic Studies* 9(1):58–73.

Strøm, Kaare. 1990. *Minority Government and Majority Rule*. Cambridge, UK: Cambridge University Press.

Strøm, Kaare. 1998. "Parliamentary Committees in European Democracies." *Journal of Legislative Studies* 4(1):21–59.

Strøm, Kaare, Wolfgang C. Müller, and Daniel Markham Smith. 2010. "Parliamentary Control of Coalition Governments." *Annual Review of Political Science* 13: 517–35.

Sumner Maine, Sir Henry. 1885. *Popular Government*. London: Murray.

Sundell, Anders. 2014. "Understanding Informal Payments in the Public Sector: Theory and Evidence from Nineteenth-Century Sweden." *Scandinavian Political Studies* 37(2):95–122.

Svahn, John A., and Mary Ross. 1983. "Social Security Amendments of 1983: Legislative History and Summary of Provisions." *Social Security Bulletin* 46(7):3–48.

Svallfors, Stefan. 2011. "A Bedrock of Support? Trends in Welfare State Attitudes in Sweden, 1981–2010." *Social Policy and Administration* 45(7):806–25.

Szakonyi, David, and Johannes Urpelainen. 2014. "Veto Players and the Value of Political Control." *Comparative Political Studies* 47(10):1384–415.

Tarrow, Sidney. 1998. *Power in Movement*, 2nd edn. Cambridge, UK: Cambridge University Press.

Tilly, Charles. 1986. *The Contentious French*. Cambridge, MA: Belknap Press of Harvard University Press.

Timmermans, Arco, and Catherine Moury. 2006. "Coalition Governance in Belgium and The Netherlands." *Acta Politica* 41(4):389–407.

Tingsten, Herbert. 1926. *Konstitutionella fullmaktslagar i modern parlamentarism*. Lund: Gleerup.

Tingsten, Herbert. 1930. *Regeringsmaktens expansion under och efter världskriget: Studier över konstitutionell fullmaktslagstifning*. Lund: Gleerup.

Tollison, Robert D., and Thomas D. Willett. 1979. "An Economic Theory of Mutually Advantageous Issue Linkages in International Negotiations." *International Organization* 33(4):425–49.

Tommasi, Mariano, Carlos Scartascini, and Ernsto Stein. 2014. "Veto Players and Policy Adaptability." *Journal of Theoretical Politics* 26(2):222–48.

Torfing, Jacob. 1999. "Workfare with Welfare." *Journal of European Social Policy* 9(1): 5–28.

Trebilcock, Michael J. 2014. *Dealing with Losers*. Oxford: Oxford University Press.

Tsebelis, George. 1990. *Nested Games*. Berkeley: University of California Press.

Tsebelis, George. 1995. "Decision Making in Political Systems: Veto Players in Presidentialism, Parliamentarism, Multicameralism, and Multipartyism." *British Journal of Political Science* 25(3):289–326.

Tsebelis, George. 1999. "Veto Players and Law Production in Parliamentary Democracies." *American Political Science Review* 93(3):591–608.

Tsebelis, George. 2000. "Veto Players and Institutional Analysis." *Governance* 13(4):441–74.

Tsebelis, George. 2002. *Veto Players*. Princeton: Princeton University Press.

Tsebelis, George. 2010. "Veto Player Theory and Policy Change: An Introduction." In *Reform Processes and Policy Change*, ed. Thomas König, George Tsebelis, and Marc Debus, 3–18. New York: Springer.

Tsebelis, George, and Hyeonho Hahm. 2014. "Suspending Vetoes: How the Euro Countries Achieved Unanimity in the Fiscal Compact." *Journal of European Public Policy* 21(10):1388–411.

Tsebelis, George, and Jeannette Money. 1997. *Bicameralism*. Cambridge, UK: Cambridge University Press.

United States Social Security Administration. 2012a. *Social Security Programs throughout the World: Asia and the Pacific, 2012*. Washington, DC: United States Social Security Administration.

United States Social Security Administration. 2012b. *Social Security Programs throughout the World: Europe, 2012*. Washington, DC: United States Social Security Administration.

United States Social Security Administration. 2013. *Social Security Programs throughout the World: The Americas, 2013*. Washington, DC: United States Social Security Administration.

Van der Linden, Bruno, (ed.). 1997. *Chômage*. Paris: De Boeck Université.

Vandenbroucke, Frank, and Kim Lievens. 2016. "Belgium." Country-specific supplement to CEPS Special Report 137, Brussels Centre for European Policy Studies.

Vandenbroucke, Frank, Chris Luigjes, Donna Wood, and Kim Lievens. 2016. "Institutional Moral Hazard in the Multi-tiered Regulation of Unemployment and Social Assistance Benefits and Activation." CEPS Special Report 137. Brussels: Centre for European Policy Studies.

Viebrock, Elke, and Jochen Clasen. 2009. "Flexicurity and Welfare Reform." *Socio-Economic Review* 7(2):305–31.

Vis, Barbara. 2009. "Governments and Unpopular Social Policy Reform." *European Journal of Political Research* 48(1):31–57.

*Wall Street Journal*. 2008. "In Crisis, Opportunity for Obama." November 21, p. A2.

Warren, Mark E., and Jane Mansbridge. 2013. "Deliberative Negotiation." In *Negotiating Agreement in Politics*, ed. Jane Mansbridge and Cathie Jo Martin, 86–120. Washington, DC: American Political Science Association.

Weingast, Barry R. 1995. "The Economic Role of Political Institutions." *Journal of Law, Economics, and Organization* 11(1):1–31.

Weishaupt, Timo. 2011. *From the Manpower Revolution to the Activation Paradigm*. Amsterdam: Amsterdam University Press.

Weisstanner, David. 2016. "The Fiscal Benefits of Repeated Cooperation: Coalitions and Debt Dynamics in 36 Democracies". *Journal of Public Policy*. DOI: 10.1017/S0143814X16000040.

Weyland, Kurt. 1998. "Swallowing the Bitter Pill: Sources of Popular Support for Neoliberal Reform in Latin America." *Comparative Political Studies* 31(5):539–68.

Wicksell, Knut. 1987 [1896]. *Om en ny princip för rättvis beskattning*. Stockholm: Ratio. The English translation, "A New Principle of Just Taxation," was published in R. A. Musgrave and A. T. Peacock (eds), *Classics in the Theory of Public Finance* (London: Macmillan, 1958).

Williams, Philip M. 1964. *Crisis and Compromise*, 3rd edn. London: Longman.

Williams, Philip M., and Martin Harrison. 1961. *De Gaulle's Republic*, 2nd edn. London: Longman.

Williams, Philip M., and Martin Harrison. 1971. *Politics and Society in de Gaulle's Republic*. London: Longman.

# Index

audience costs 38, 47, 51, 55–7, 62, 70–2, 74n
  definition of 55

Belgium 48, 57–62, 70–1
bicameralism 26, 41, 54–5
bureaucracy 8, 38, 49, 52, 64–5, 70, 77–9, 103
  in the United States 72

central banks 8, 51, 138
Christian democratic parties 7, 59
coalition government 1, 6–8, 25, 40, 41n, 55, 64–6, 70, 82–3, 137
  and fiscal policy 66–9
  and labor market reform 35–7, 90–1
  in Belgium and the Netherlands 59–62
  in France 99
  in Switzerland 7, 97
commitment problems 25, 47–8, 62–3, 69–72, 74, 81, 87, 88, 96, 98, 105, 111, 124n, 132
  long-run 39, 64–9, 78, 82–3, 115–16
  short-run 38, 63–4, 77
committees. See legislatures, committees in
communism 13–14, 100n
compensation, definition of 22
compromise, definition of 23
concentration-of-power hypothesis, the 1, 3, 6, 8–9, 11n, 12, 26, 43n, 131
consensual democracy 2, 6, 9–10, 135. See also power sharing
corporatism 64, 102, 111
  definition of 8
  in the Netherlands 60, 71
  in Sweden 97n
corruption 17, 52, 57, 70
courts, political role of 7–8, 51–2, 63, 72

deadweight costs 38, 47, 49–52, 62, 70–2, 74n, 76
  definition of 49
delegation 7–8, 51, 64–5, 70–1, 138–9
deliberation 2, 8, 10, 12, 56–7, 136
democratic paralysis 1, 5–6, 10, 11n, 14, 16, 20, 33, 38, 47, 53, 55n, 69, 71, 74, 88, 106, 113, 132, 135–6

definition of 5
  in the United States 48, 72
Denmark 27, 57
dilution costs 24, 38, 47–52, 62, 70, 72, 74n
  definition of 49
disasters. See natural disasters
divided government 1, 11, 26n, 55
  definition of 25
  in the United States 71–3
drift 3, 16

economic crises 4, 13n, 30, 34, 71, 123, 125
economic policy 2, 8, 18, 30, 124. See also fiscal policy
economic view of politics, as opposed to religious view 13–14, 42n
Ecuador 56–7
electoral systems. See majoritarian democracy and proportional democracy
European Union, the 32–3, 50n, 51–2, 100, 137–8

Finland 57
fiscal capacity. See tax policy
fiscal policy 4–5, 28, 42, 48, 51, 53, 66–9, 71, 124
France 33n, 85, 91–6, 98–100, 105
  employment protection in 94–5, 98–9
  Fifth Republic in 91–2, 99–100
  Fourth Republic in 5, 92, 99, 123
  pension reforms in 93–5, 98, 119
  unemployment insurance in 30

Germany 33n, 97, 119
  bicameralism in 54
  judicial appointments in 52
  Weimar Republic in 6, 123
good government 3, 134–7
governability 5n, 16
government debt. See fiscal policy
Greece 33
gridlock 5, 19n, 71, 73n, 138. See also democratic paralysis

Printed and bound by CPI Group (UK) Ltd, Croydon, CR0 4YY